EDIBLE INSECTS

Edible

Series Editor: Andrew F. Smith

EDIBLE is a revolutionary series of books dedicated to food and drink that explores the rich history of cuisine. Each book reveals the global history and culture of one type of food or beverage.

Already published

Edible Insects

A Global History

Gina Louise Hunter

REAKTION BOOKS

Published by Reaktion Books Ltd
Unit 32, Waterside
44–48 Wharf Road
London N1 7UX, UK
www.reaktionbooks.co.uk

First published 2021
Copyright © Gina Louise Hunter 2021

Printed and bound in India by Replika Press Pvt. Ltd

A catalogue record for this book is available from the British Library

ISBN 978 1 78914 446 8

Contents

Introduction

Insects are vital to human life. They decompose our waste, pollinate our crops and control agricultural pests. They provide us with treasured products such as honey, wax, silk, colourful dyes (carmine) and polishes (shellac). Insects are used in medicine. Ant mandibles once served as sutures, and fly maggots are still used for wound debridement. Insects are admired for their beauty. They are used for adornment, such as beetlewing art and jewellery, and they have provided motifs and imagery since the earliest forms of artistry.

Some insects are kept as pets or bred for sport. In China, the keeping of 'singing' crickets and breeding of fighting crickets dates to antiquity. Feared and revered, insects have been a font of human symbolism and spirituality. Among the ancient Egyptians, the scarab beetle was the divine manifestation of Khepri, the morning sun god. For the ancient Greeks, a moth signified the goddess Psyche and the soul. For Hebrews, Beelzebub, the Lord of the Flies, was Satan himself. For Buddhists, the cicada symbolizes resurrection. For Native Americans in southern California, the ingestion of red harvester ants provided visions and access to supernatural powers. Among Jains in India, for whom all life is sacred, the principle of *ahimsa* (non-violence) compels the most devout to sweep the ground in front of them as they walk so as not to crush an insect and to cover their mouths lest one fly in and perish.

Entomophagy, the intentional consumption of insects, is only one way humans have relied on them, and we have done so since the dawn of humanity. We eat insects because

An example of beetlewing embroidery from 19th-century India. The leaves are made of beetle elytra (hard wings).

A carved cricket container from China of unknown date.

they are nutritious, and because they taste good. Some insects provide abundant sustenance. Other insects are occasional delicacies or offer intense seasoning. Usually, insects supplement other fare: a few bugs collected with berries and a nut here and there – the original trail mix. Other insects, such as silkworm pupae, are an edible by-product of another human–insect endeavour.

My favourite insect food is *escamoles*, the Mexican 'caviar of the desert'. They resemble petite white beans or pine nuts but taste like young sweetcorn kernels cut from the cob and drenched in butter. Due to their appearance, escamoles are sometimes referred to as ant 'eggs', but they are actually the larvae and pupae of the *Liometopum apiculatum* ant. They are native to parts of Mexico and the southwestern United States, where their nests can be found below ground at the base of certain desert plants.

In Mexico, escamoles are considered a delicacy. Fried with chillies, garlic and onion, they are served with tortillas or

Modern replica of a blue scarab beetle figure, used as amulets and impression seals in ancient Egypt.

on their own. Appreciation of them dates to pre-Hispanic times. Their name derives from the native Nahuatl word *azcamolli*, which refers to ant stew. For the Aztecs, escamoles were tribute food presented to their emperor Moctezuma II (*r.* 1502–20) on special occasions. Today they fetch a high price in upmarket restaurants in Mexico City and other urban centres. The price reflects their limited, seasonal availability (from February to April), as well as the difficulty involved in their harvest.

People who find and harvest this treat are called *escamoleros*; they brave biting black ants to excavate the brood from nests. A skilled *escamolero* knows to harvest only part of the nest, leaving behind enough larvae to regenerate the colony. A careful harvest allows the same nest to be revisited for forty years or more. The high demand for escamoles, however, provides an incentive for unskilled poachers to over-harvest and destroy the nests, which has resulted in a precipitous decline of the ant population. The idea of eating ant larvae may be repulsive to some people, but I might eat them more often if they were available outside of Mexico and I was not worried about their over-exploitation. They are delicious.

Like most North Americans, I did not grow up eating insects, at least not intentionally. Western culture has long rejected insect foods, but we are in the minority. Insects have been relished foodstuffs for most of the world's cultures. In fact, an estimated 2 billion people in societies across the world today regularly consume insects.[1]

If the thought of tucking into a bowl of stir-fried insects makes you shudder, consider the fact that you already eat

Prepared escamoles, ant larvae and pupae (*Liometopum apiculatum*).

insect-derived ingredients all the time. Carmine, a natural red food colourant derived from the scale insect, cochineal (*Dactylopius coccus*), is common in yoghurts, juices, confectionery and cakes. Shellac, a resin secreted by the female lac bug (*Kerria lacca*), provides the glaze on pharmaceutical pills and confections; it adds shelf-life and sheen to your citrus fruits and apples.

We all also frequently consume whole insects and insect parts unintentionally because they are impossible to remove entirely from our foodstuffs. They are found in our fresh fruits, vegetables and grains, and they end up in our processed foods. Governments set limits on the allowable amount of insect 'defects' and 'filth'. According to the u.s. Food and Drug Administration's *Food Defect Levels Handbook*, peanut butter may have up to thirty insect fragments per 100 grams (⅓–½ u.s. cup), and 50 grams (¼ cup) of wheat flour may have up to 75 insect fragments.[2] Consumers are none the worse for this 'contamination' however (except perhaps those with allergies).

For most in the West, the intentional consumption of insects is limited to exotic dining events, entomology festivals, 'extreme' food TV shows, survivalists' guidebooks and travellers' adventures. Recently, however, insect foods appear

One species of lac insect (*Tachardiella fulgens*) on a branch in Arizona.

to be going mainstream. European and North American grocery stores and food shops now stock new insect-based food products, and a small cadre of chefs and entrepreneurs have set out to convince sceptical Western consumers that a bug can be a tasty bite. Newspaper and magazine headlines call insects 'superfoods' and the 'hottest new food trend'. Meanwhile, food security experts have argued that insects are the key to sustainable and plentiful protein for future generations while also providing avenues for economic development.[3] New mass-rearing systems have been set up in several countries allowing for industrial-scale insect food production.

Should we all include a few more bugs in our diet? Are insects really nutritious, and if so, why do they provoke such disgust in some of us? How have the world's diverse cultures utilized insects for food? Are insects more sustainably raised than other animals? Will increased trade in wild-caught insects provide income and food security for marginalized populations? This book examines these and other questions.

Although often considered an under-studied topic, the literature on insects as human food is vast and often complex for those, like me, who are not trained in entomology. Nevertheless, as your hostess and chef in the chapters ahead, I serve up a carefully selected tasting menu of edible insects from around the world. It is not a smorgasbord, for the range of insect foods is very large. Instead, I offer some especially tasty portions: stories of insect eating from around the world, local preparation habits, and even a recipe or two in case you want to try them yourself. On the menu are meats, mostly wild-caught, a few farmed. I even have some home-raised varieties to share. I invite you to a seat at the table. Bon appétit!

Goliath birdeater tarantula (*Theraphosa blondi*).

I

Insects as Human Food

The Goliath birdeater tarantula (*Theraphosa blondi*) is the world's largest spider, as large as a dinner plate. To encounter it, photographer Peter Menzel and his wife, Faith D'Aluisio, travelled up the Orinoco River to a small village in the Venezuelan Amazon. From there, indigenous Yanomami boys took the couple tarantula hunting in the forest. Hunting for these spiders entailed sticking the ends of braided vines into underground tunnels where the spiders live until they grab hold of the braid and can be pulled out. After many hours of searching, a large *T. blondi* was captured. Back at the village, a boy stunned the tarantula by whacking it with a machete and then lowered it into a fire. As its insides cooked, it let out a hiss and a squirt of hot fluid a metre (3 ft) long. After seven minutes of roasting, they rubbed off the charred hairs, pulled off the legs and found white meat inside that tasted something like smoked crab. This great story comes from the couple's award-winning book *Man Eating Bugs: The Art and Science of Eating Insects* (1998). The cover features a charming Cambodian woman munching on a smaller (but just as scary-looking) species of tarantula.[1]

It must really bug the entomologists among us that a book dedicated to insects features a spider on the cover!

Scientifically speaking, spiders are arachnids, not insects. In the folk taxonomy of many people, however, several taxonomically distinct orders of creepy crawly creatures are all lumped together under the general category of insects, or *bugs* to the average North American.

What Is an Insect?

The word 'bug', in English, dates to ancient times and once referred to ghosts – those frequently hard to see, frightening (or at least highly unpleasant) beings that lurk and pester. It is not hard to understand why the reference was later transferred to insects. The word 'insect' came into the English language in 1601, in a translation of Pliny the Elder's *Natural History*.[2] Like Aristotle of centuries before, Pliny developed a system of classifying the natural world. *Insect* comes from the Latin 'cut into', referring to the segments of an insect's body. *Entoma*, the root of *entomology* (the study of insects), is Greek for the same thing. Their segmented bodies are one defining characteristic. The classification system currently used by scientists to name living creatures comes from Carl Linnaeus, a Swedish botanist, whose binomial (two-name) nomenclature is based on similarity of form, with each species belonging to a genus and genera arranged into larger and more diverse categories of families, orders, classes, phyla and, finally, kingdoms.

Insects are part of the animal kingdom, members of the phylum Arthropoda (from *arthro*, jointed, and *poda*, foot), which includes other intertebrate (without a backbone) creatures with jointed appendages and an exoskeleton (an external skeleton). Arthropods include many subcategories (or subphyla) such as crustaceans, earthworms and leeches spiders and scorpions, centipedes and millipedes. Insects belong to their own taxonomic class, Insecta, whose major distinguishing features are three major body divisions with three pairs of legs attached to the thorax. They are also the only arthropods (in fact the only invertebrates) that sometimes have wings.

So, to be taxonomically accurate, an insect is a small invertebrate animal that, as an adult, possesses the following characteristics: 1. a hardened exoskeleton; 2. three (usually) distinct body parts (head, thorax and abdomen); 3. one pair of segmented antennae; 4. one pair of compound eyes (in most cases); 5. three pairs of segmented legs, with one pair on each of three thoracic segments; and 6. usually one or two pairs of wings, although some adults are wingless.

One amazing fact about insects is that they are the dominant form of life on earth. Scientists have identified over 1 million species *so far*. By comparison, there are only 6,495 known mammals.[3] Entomologists agree that there are millions of yet-to-be identified insect species, but estimates of exactly how many more vary tremendously, from 4 million to as many as 30 million more species.[4]

How Many Are Edible?

The number of potentially edible insect species is unknown. Professor Yde Jongema, an entomologist at Wageningen University in the Netherlands, maintains a list of insect species known to have been used as human food around the world. The task is complex since many records that mention insect consumption lack specific taxonomic information. Jongema's most up-to-date list contains 2,111 edible species (this list includes spiders and other arthropods).[5]

The vast majority of scientifically classified edible insect species belong to five orders (known as the 'big five'):

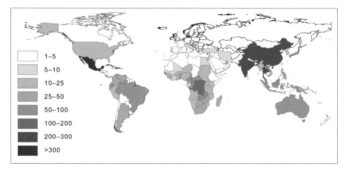

Recorded edible insect species by country.

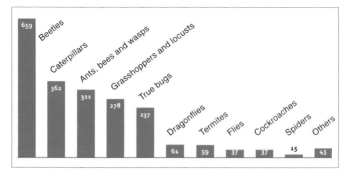

Number of recorded edible insects per group in the world.

Coleoptera (the beetle order, which boasts 659 known edible species); Lepidoptera (the butterfly and moth order, with 362 edible species); Hymenoptera (ants, bees and wasps, 321 edible species); Orthoptera (grasshoppers, crickets and katydids, 278 species); and Hemiptera (the order of 'true' bugs, such as stink bugs and cicadas, 237 edible species).

Many edible insect species are only eaten (or are preferred) during certain developmental stages, so it is important to understand a bit about insect life cycles. After hatching from eggs, insects develop by moulting, or shedding their hard, outer cuticle layer and expanding their tissues before

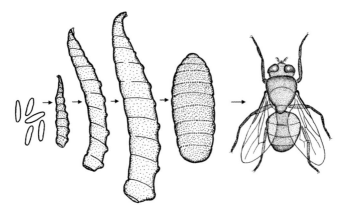

Complete metamorphosis of the housefly life cycle from egg through three larval instars to pupa to adult.

the new cuticle hardens. This can happen four to eight (or even more) times; these immature, developing insects are called instars. The immatures (or nymphs) of some insects, such as grasshoppers, look like miniature versions of the adults and generally subsist on the same food as the adults. Other insects undergo complete metamorphosis into adulthood. Species of the butterfly and moth order Lepidoptera, for instance, mature from egg to larva (caterpillar) to pupa (chrysalis) to adult. The appearance and behaviour of the insect differs dramatically at these stages, and so does their potential use for human food.

The developmental stage of an insect determines its edibility and nutrient composition, as well as how it is collected and prepared. Butterfly and moth species are most frequently consumed in the caterpillar stage rather than in their winged adult stage.

Where Are Insects Consumed?

While the human consumption of insects is often called entomophagy, a related term, 'insectivory', is generally reserved for dietary patterns of non-human animals that subsist primarily on insects. Whereas some non-human animals (and even some plants such as the Venus flytrap) are insectivorous, humans are omnivorous: that is, we are able to subsist on a wide variety of plants and animals. Entomophagy thus usually refers to a human food choice. Some writers also use the cumbersome 'anthropoentomophagy'.[6]

The consumption of insects is widespread throughout the world. Insects are eaten by 3,071 different ethnic groups in 130 countries.[7] Generally, more insect species are consumed in tropical than temperate regions because there is greater biodiversity in the tropics and therefore a greater chance of finding a tasty bug. The significance of insects in people's diets and the manner in which they are consumed vary by species and locale. The use and significance of insects in the human diet is both a biogeographic and a cultural phenomenon.

Role of Insect Foods in Human Evolution

It was in 1960, in Gombe National Park, Tanzania, that the primatologist Jane Goodall first watched a chimpanzee snap a twig and peel all the leaves off. Eyeing a nearby termite mound, the chimpanzee dipped the twig into the termite hole for a moment before withdrawing it, now covered with termites. The termites promptly became a tasty snack for the lucky chimpanzee. Goodall's revolutionary observations of chimpanzee tools erased the then-prevalent idea that tool-making is a uniquely human trait, and chimps have since been observed 'fishing' for termites with grass, leaves and sticks modified expressly for this purpose.

Chimpanzees use a variety of tools and techniques to obtain insect foods. Humans have similar tools for harvesting them. We probably both inherited our taste for them from our common ancestor who wandered the earth some 5–6 million years ago. Indeed, some of the earliest tools we have found with hominins, a term that refers to our direct ancestors as well as to various extinct bipedal relatives, are for insect gathering. The Australopithecines, who lived in Africa from 4.2 to 1.5 million years ago, devised bone tools to dig into termite mounds.[8]

Studies of chimpanzees at Gombe have shown that termite-fishing behaviour is especially important for females.[9] In fact, female chimpanzees who more frequently fish for termites have greater reproductive success than those who do so less often. Chimpanzees are known to occasionally kill

Chimpanzee using a stick tool to catch food from a termite hole.

and eat vertebrates, but males often dominate access to this meat. Termite fishing may be the way that female chimps ensure adequate nutrition for themselves and their offspring.

Anthropologist Julie Lesnik studies the role of tool use and insect foods (especially those tasty termites) in the diets of early hominins as well as in the diets of contemporary insect-gatherers. Lesnik hypothesizes that our early human ancestors ate significant amounts of insects because they were abundant in the tropical forest and savanna environments in which humans evolved and because insects are relatively less risky to obtain compared to hunting other animals.[10] She and other researchers believe that insects and their by-products (such as honey) were probably very important food sources for our human ancestors.[11] In particular, insects may have been crucial protein sources for reproductive females who may have followed a tried and true hominin subsistence strategy by relying on edible insects to meet their increased nutritional needs.

Modern humans (*Homo sapiens*) appeared in Africa some 200,000 years ago, and for most of our existence, we hunted and gathered wild foods for our sustenance. (Agriculture dates to only 13,000 years ago.) Anthropologists often look to historical cases of foraging societies to make inferences about the lifeways of our prehistoric ancestors. The image of a Stone Age 'Man [*sic*], the hunter', with his stone axes, spears and big game, is misleading; historical examples of foragers show that gathered foods are often more important in the diet. These foraging societies had a gender-based division of labour whereby men hunted more often, and had greater access to meat, than women; while women and children more frequently gathered foods, including insects. Our evolutionary history perhaps explains the special importance of insects in women's diets.

Some of the most famously studied foragers are the San people of southern Africa. Lesnik has spent time with contemporary San and believes early researchers likely underestimated the role of insects in the San diet perhaps because insects are often collected by women and children and eaten on the spot, making it more difficult for researchers to adequately assess their contribution to the overall diet.[12] Western researchers have also assumed that insects were an emergency food, or a food of last resort scrounged to ward off starvation and abandoned once 'better' food was available, but this is erroneous. Lesnik notes that insects are relished items that San women go out of their way to collect. San take advantage of insects available all year round as well as seasonal resources. One seasonally available insect that is especially important is the caterpillar of a hawk moth species (Sphingidae). When these caterpillars appear, San women set up camp near their host trees and collect caterpillars to roast and dry. These can be kept for months and are just one of eighteen edible insect species that the San collect.

Nutritional Profile of Insects

It is no wonder that so many people have made use of insect foods. Insects are a nutritional powerhouse. Like other animal meats, insects are composed of fats, proteins and a variety of micro-nutrients. Many insects are more nutritious gram for gram than contemporary protein sources like beef or chicken. One hundred grams (3 ½ oz) of cricket protein offers about the same protein content gram for gram as beef and pork but only half the fat content and more iron and calcium. The following table provides a comparison of insects with some common animal foods (beef, chicken and pork).[13]

The nutritional profile of different insect species varies widely. The protein content of 100 grams of silkworm pupae is 14.8 grams (½ oz) but is as high as 35 grams (1¼ oz) for mopane worms. The average fat content per 100 grams of honeybee brood (larvae and pupae) is only 3.64 grams (⅛ oz), but is 25.3 grams (just under 1 oz) for palm weevil.

It is hard to know exactly what kind of nutrition one will get from a serving of, say, termites. For many species, reliable and comparable data are simply nonexistent. Furthermore, entomologist Charlotte Payne and her colleagues in the UK and Japan analysed samples of insects acquired on the market and found great variation of nutritional profile *within* a single insect species. In other words, some of the cricket samples they acquired were more nutritious than others. This variation is likely due to differing environmental conditions, such as the richness of an insect's habitat, or the quality of feed given to farmed insects. The nutrient profile of conventional meats also depends on a number of factors such as breed and feed.[14]

One special feature that adult insects offer that other meats do not is fibre in the form of chitin (pronounced ky-tin).

Termite mound, Democratic Republic of Congo.

Source (values are for edible portion)	Kcal (per 100 g)	Protein (g)	Fat (g)	Iron (g)	Calcium (mg)
RNI/RV/UL					
Beef	176	20	10	1.95	5
Chicken	120	22.5	2.62	0.88	8
Pork	142	19.8	6.34	0.8	7
Cricket (adult)	153	20.1	5.06	5.46	104
Honeybee (brood)	499	15.2	3.64	18.5	30
Silkworm (pupae)	128	14.8	8.26	1.8	42
Mopane caterpillar	409	35.2	15.2	—	700
Palm weevil (larvae)	479	9.96	25.3	2.58	39.6
Mealworm (larvae)	247	19.4	12.3	1.87	42.9

Nutritional comparison of common edible insects and conventional meats.

Chitin is the principal structural component of an arthropod's exoskeleton. It is generally considered an insoluble fibre, the kind of fibre that most people do not digest but that creates bulk in the intestines. However, some people from societies that habitually eat insects possess an enzyme (chitonase) that is capable of degrading chitin. There is recent evidence that chitin (for instance, in the form of whole-cricket powder) is a prebiotic that when ingested can increase the intestinal microbiota, improving gut health and reducing systemic inflammation.[15]

Swarms and Social Insects

You might be wondering how you would ever acquire enough termites to fill you up. Indeed, the majority of insects are small in comparison to most of the animals that humans eat, but some swarm or live in nests and can be collected in great quantities. We know that, historically, swarming insects provided ample food to some foragers. Archaeologist Mark Q. Sutton collected historical accounts of insects in the diets of foragers of the Great Basin region of the western United States. Native Americans in this region hunted game and gathered pinyon seeds but also took rich and easy sustenance from periodic locust swarms. As locusts descended on the Great Salt Lake, they would perish in the saline water and wash up on the shore in long windrows. In one calculation, 'American Indians gathered locusts from the shores of the Great Salt Lake and acquired 10 times more calories per hour than they did by hunting big game and nearly 300 times more than they did by collecting seeds.'[16]

Social insects (ants, bees and termites) live in colonies (such as a beehive) that can also provide a large cache of ready insect food. Colonies are divided into castes, whose members differ in form, function and behaviour. Reproductive caste members (for instance, a queen bee and male drones) differ from steriles (like worker bees). In an integrated and intergenerational colony, each caste plays a distinct role, such as foraging, food storage, nest maintenance, care of nymphs, defence or reproduction. Castes differ in their seasonal availability, their behaviour and their nutritional profile and those who gather social insects make use of their predictable characteristics. Some societies were thought to rely so heavily on termites and honeybees that they were called termite or honey 'civilizations'.[17]

Termites

Termites (*Macrotermes* spp.) are a vital food source for people in Africa, Asia and Latin America today. Although there are some 48 termite species known to be eaten worldwide, the most consumed belong to the genus *Macrotermes*, and in particular the species, *Macrotermes bellicosus*.[18] Large colonies of *Macrotermes* are found in arid areas of Central and East Africa and are harvested seasonally during the rainy season, when reproductive members of the colonies swarm and take flight.

Like other social insects, the nutritional value of termites varies by species as well as by developmental stage and caste. In termite colonies, adult male and female reproductive members with wings, called *alates*, leave the nest to mate and start new colonies. Alates and nymphs (immature termites), which are available only seasonally, generally have high fat content. Soldier termites, which are available year-round, have less fat but offer higher protein content. The soldier caste of a *Syntermes* species found in Venezuela, for example, have a remarkable protein content of 64 per cent.[19]

Alates and nymphs are the most commonly eaten termite castes, followed by soldier castes that remain inside the mound and must be fished out if they are to be eaten. Queens are also sometimes eaten but this is less common because it entails the difficult work of destroying the termite mound to find them. Termite queens are usually a prized delicacy reserved for special occasions but, in Uganda and Zambia, they are recognized as especially nutritious and fed to undernourished children.

The flying reproductive alates are easily collected in several ways. One way is to place an upside-down basket, or a dome-shaped frame of sticks covered in cloth, over the hole from which the alates emerge. Sometimes the ground is drummed or beaten to simulate rain, which provokes the alates to exit their nests. Termite alates are also attracted to light and so are easy to attract in the evening with a lantern or, these days, an electric light, placed above a pail of water, which traps the insects.[20] Sometimes termites are stripped of their wings and eaten raw on the spot, but more often they are boiled and dried, fried lightly (no oil needed since they have plenty of their own fat) or smoked and steamed in banana leaves.[21]

Soldier termites can be collected in much the same way that chimpanzees 'fish' for termites. In rural South Africa, Julie Lesnik accompanied women as they collected soldier termites from mounds known to be productive. These women break open a mound and insert a loose grass broom into the nest. When they withdraw the broom, soldier termites cling to the grasses and with a swift swipe of a closed hand can be transferred to a plastic bucket. Skill is needed because these soldier termites have a mean bite. The women take their pails of termites home to be rinsed, boiled with salt and placed in a basket to dry. Later, the women sell these treats in the market. Lesnik, who has tried many insects, says these are her favourite – they taste like popcorn.

Termite harvest.

A termite hunter offers a taste of his catch, Kenya, 2017.

There are plenty of other ways of preparing and using termites. In the Democratic Republic of the Congo and the Central African Republic, for instance, the fat from termites is squeezed into a tube and used as an oil for frying. In Botswana, the alates of the harvester termite *Hodotermes mossambicus* are roasted in hot ash and sand before being consumed. In Kenya, termites are roasted or sun-dried and then ground and mixed with other ingredients to produce termite crackers and muffins.[22]

Although there are more cases of edible termites in Africa than elsewhere, the use of termites as food (and sometimes as medicine) has been recorded in 29 countries over three continents. In Brazil, one species has been used in traditional medicine to treat asthma, sinusitis and other diseases. In

Nigeria, another species is used to treat wounds and morning sickness, and as a charm for spiritual protection. Scientific studies have shown that termites have antibiotic and anti-fungal properties that could be therapeutic for humans.[23]

Bees

As Pliny the Elder once said, 'Among them all, the first rank, and our especial admiration, ought, in justice, to be accorded to bees, which alone, of all the insects, have been created for the benefit of man.'[24] Honey is universally consumed and appreciated, but bees also provide wax and propolis. In some cases, bee brood and adult bees themselves are eaten. Although we think of it mainly as a sweet condiment or ingredient, honey has been a substantial dietary component for some peoples, especially hunters and gatherers. The Mbuti forest people of the Congo, for instance, were said to derive 80 per cent of their dietary energy from honey during its season,[25] but the season lasts only two months.[26] Along with honey itself, bee brood (larvae and pupae in the comb) were often consumed.

Among the most famous honey gatherers historically were the hunters and gatherers of Sri Lanka, who would go to extraordinary lengths to secure the most prized honeys. The prolific entomologist F. S. Bodenheimer (1897–1959) called Sri Lankan forest dwellers a 'honey civilization' and wrote that honey-hunting was '*the* master art of the Vedda'.[27] These forest dwellers were skilled at following bees back to their nests and extracting hives with specialized tools. Of the many species of bees and their honey in Sri Lanka, the most desired and difficult to obtain is that of the *bambara* (*Apis dorsata*), a very aggressive bee. The acquisition of these hives

Bee brood of the western honeybee (*Apis mellifera*).

was thus only for the young and valiant, who would undertake their harvests at night when the bees were less active. Bambara build nests on the precipitous sides of cliffs. To access these, the hunters constructed vine ladders with rungs and secured these to a tree above the cliff. The brave hunter would be lowered over the cliff with the various tools he would need roped onto his arms: four leaf-bundle torches (*hulas*), a double-ended forked prong and a deerskin bag for the harvest. At the base of the cliff, supporters would build a fire and sing, and on the cliff guarding the ropes above was only the hunter's most trusted peer. Bodenheimer writes,

> Imagine then the picture of the man smothered in smoke, assailed by angry bees, swinging in the darkness 70 m. or more above the stony earth, with neck and knee hitched to the ladder so as to leave the arms free to manipulate torch and prong. Is it a wonder that not every Vedda is a *kapunkaraya*, a cutter, but only the

boldest of them? And that when climbing down to his work, he does so with the thought in his heart that he now has no use for life or father or mother?[28]

The heroic harvest and the great pain and exhaustion of the hero provided food for these foragers but also a preservative for meats; they were known to put raw meat into a hollowed log which was then filled with honey to seal out air and contaminants.

Another 'honey civilization', according to Bodenheimer's accounts, were the Guayaki Indians of eastern Paraguay, for whom honey provided a basic food, 'much more important to them than hunting or even vegetable products'.[29] While the idea of a civilization based on a staple of honey may be exaggerated, honey probably did play a larger role in pre-industrial diets than is usually acknowledged.[30]

Why Do Some People Find Insects Disgusting?

Because humans are omnivores and can derive sustenance from a huge variety of foods, culture plays the principal role in determining what is good to eat. The willingness to try novel foods is most likely an evolutionary adaptation that helps humans get the most nutrition out of the resources at hand. This is countered by a level of wariness about unfamiliar and unproven foods that may be harmful to us. This balance between neophilia (the desire for new foods) and neophobia (the reluctance to try new foods) varies among cultures, among individuals and over a person's life.

For many in the West, it feels 'only natural' that one would avoid eating bugs, spiders and other creepy crawly creatures.

In fact, our avoidance of insects is more cultural than biological, although there is some evidence that a fear of certain animals may be adaptive. Some experimental research has shown, for instance, that monkeys are intrinsically primed to acquire a fear of snakes. In one study, laboratory monkeys who had never seen a snake quickly learned to respond to them with fear after seeing videos of their wild peers displaying fearful reactions to snakes.[31] However, when the videotapes were manipulated to show wild monkeys panicking at the sight of other creatures, such as rabbits and flowers, the captive monkeys did not learn the fear. Only certain snakes are venomous and potentially dangerous, but a generalized fear of all snakes may have evolved as a protective mechanism against the ones that are life-threatening.

One might expect, then, that something similar occurs with insects, that humans are evolutionarily predisposed to fear insects because some of them are potentially harmful, but there is actually little evidence for this. Arachnophobia (fear of spiders), for instance, is commonplace in the West, but less common among people of non-Western origin; and there is no evidence that non-human primates are predisposed to fear spiders.[32] In fact, Western entomophobia (and arachnophobia) is out of proportion to the peril that the majority of these creatures pose and our fears are usually misplaced. Most spiders are harmless, even beneficial, to humans. We ought rather to fear mosquitoes, as they are far more dangerous to human health than spiders. Mosquitoes are indirectly responsible for 750,000 deaths worldwide each year, mostly in tropical areas, via their transmission of malaria and other diseases. In the u.s., where mosquito-borne diseases are much rarer, bees and wasps are the insects that cause the most deaths. Each year about one hundred Americans die from bee or wasp stings due to allergic reactions to their venom.

People, in fact, *do* eat even potentially harmful, scary-looking (at least to me) creatures like tarantulas, as we have seen. Tarantulas have a painful, but generally not lethal, bite. The hairs that cover their bodies, however, can irritate the mucous membranes of those who get that close. In Cambodia, tarantulas are called *a-ping* and the city of Skuon is especially famous for serving them. Some say that Cambodians turned to eating *a-ping* to avoid starvation during the Khmer Rouge regime, but the practice is probably far older. Since the 1990s, *a-ping* have been sold primarily to tourists in Skuon and other cities as a street food; they are served spiced and deep-fried and displayed in large baskets. To create a spectacle and attract shocked tourists to their wares, vendors may put whole, live, de-fanged spiders in their mouths or let them walk on their faces.

When it comes to eating insects, the emotion some experience is disgust rather than fear. According to psychologist Paul Rozin, disgust is at root a food-related emotion that focuses on our animal nature and bodily products. The

Fried spiders, Skuon, Cambodia.

experience of disgust may have originally helped humans to avoid toxic substances. For instance, 'contamination disgust' makes us concerned not only about what a potentially edible object is made of, but where it has been. Since some insects are associated with spoilage (maggots and flies), disease (parasitic worms) and dirtiness, disgust perhaps helped humans avoid pathogens through the development of hygienic behaviours.[33]

This does not easily explain Westerners' generalized aversion to insects. Few people are viscerally disgusted by things such as unwashed hands, coughing or breathing, even though they are also sources of infection. Moreover, grasshoppers, crickets, cicadas and the larvae of many insects consume only vegetable matter and thus are far cleaner than lobsters, crabs and some shrimp species, which eat carrion, yet the former are 'gross' and the latter are relished.

Perhaps our antipathy towards insects stems from 'animal reminder disgust'. This is the disgust we experience at things that remind us of our own animal nature (faeces, blood, innards) and of death. This disgust can be triggered by eating things that resemble whole animals. Thus urban Europeans and North Americans whose meat supply is far removed from slaughter may find it disgusting to eat recognizable animal parts including whole insects with identifiable parts.

Whatever its basic biological roots, the emotion of disgust has become a cultural mechanism for pushing away anything one's own culture considers offensive. Aversion to insects, and insect foods, is a product of culture, history and geography, rather than primarily biology.

It is unclear when and why the West turned away from insect foods. Some have suggested that with the advent of plant and animal domestication (and particularly in the Fertile Crescent) people slowly shifted away from eating insects and began to see them as agricultural pests.[34] However, insect foods are found in the culinary repertoire of many agricultural peoples and only certain insect species present agricultural problems. In fact, harvesting destructive species of insects, such as grasshoppers, from fields is a successful form of pest control.

Another theory is that Europe was relatively rich in other animal proteins, such that collecting smaller sources, like insects, offered a lower caloric return for the time invested in hunting and preparation. Biodiversity certainly plays a role in shaping human diet. Europe and other temperate regions have less biodiversity, fewer insects and fewer insect eaters. In fact, Europe suffered a cooling period between 1150 and 1850, called the 'Little Ice Age', and probably lost and never recovered from a previous era of greater biodiversity. This period of colder weather impacted Europe's forest species, disrupted agriculture and brought dire consequences to its populations, but whether this had any impact on insect consumption is unknown.[35]

Over time in the West, eating insects became a sign of primitiveness and of material poverty; and once symbolically and psychologically categorized as such, insects became 'bad to eat'. As anthropologist Marvin Harris explains, 'The reason we don't eat [insects] is not that they are dirty and loathsome; rather, they are dirty and loathsome because we don't eat them.'[36] There is nothing inherent about insects to provoke our disgust, and it is not shared by the millions of people today who appreciate and eat many kinds of insects.

2
A History of Insect Eating

Human use of insects as sustenance is as old as humanity. Palaeolithic (40,000–8,000 years ago) cave paintings representing honey hunting and bees have been found in India, Australia, southern Africa and Spain.[1] The most famous, from the Araña Caves in Bicorp, Valencia, dates to 7,000–15,000 years ago and depicts a human figure suspended on a ladder facing a beehive surrounded by the buzzing insects. It is an ancient representation of honey collection methods used into contemporary times. Another intriguing artefact is a bison bone engraved with the image of a cricket (*Troglophilus* spp.) dated at over 10,000 years old, found in the Trois-Frères cave in Ariège, France.

Evidence of insect consumption in the archaeological record is difficult to find and interpret because insects leave little behind and can be intrusive. Insect remains and residues left in storage pits, hearths and pots can sometimes be used to infer food storage, processing and consumption. This is the case, for instance, for large quantities of grasshoppers and other insects found in 4,600-year-old sites in the Great Basin region of the western United States. These are believed to be food caches, because they correspond to ethnographic observations of insect collection in the same

Cave drawing from Araña Cave, Bicorp, Valencia, dated 8000–6000 BC depicts a honey harvester at work.

region. Silkworm cocoons recovered from a 2,500-year-old site in Shanxi Province have holes poked into them, indicating that the pupae may have been extracted and eaten, as they are today.[2]

Direct evidence of what prehistoric humans ate comes from dental wear patterns, chemical analysis of bone and coprolites (fossilized faeces). A site in the Tehuacán Valley in Mexico, spanning a period of 8,700 to 450 years ago, includes human coprolites containing caterpillars, flies, ants, lice, fleas, ticks, beetles, bees and wasps and unidentified fragments of other insects that archaeologists concluded were used for food.[3] Fossilized grasshopper parts have been detected in

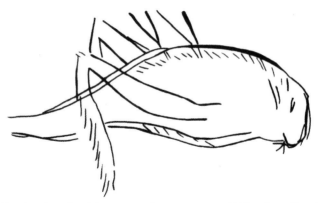

Line drawing of a cricket engraved on 10,000-year-old bison bone found at the Cave of the Trois-Frères in southwestern France.

coprolites and in hearths from numerous archaeological sites around the world. Unfortunately, insects are often overlooked in archaeological investigations.[4]

Ancient History

Ancient texts from around the world document the culinary uses of insects. The Bible mentions insect foods in the Old and New Testaments. The 'manna' that God provided for the Israelites in the desert described in the book of Exodus might be the crystallized liquid excretions of a the mealy bug (*Trabutina mannipara*) that feeds on tamarisk trees. In the Middle East today, people still collect this sweet excretion from the trees. They call it 'man'.[5]

Consumption of grasshoppers and locusts in the Middle East is an ancient habit. In Leviticus (11:20), Moses defines which insects the Hebrews are permitted to eat: 'Even these of them ye may eat: the *arbeh* [locust] after its kind, and the katydid after its kind, and the cricket after its kind, and the grasshopper after its kind' (Leviticus 11:22). One of the earliest known pieces of evidence for insect consumption is a bas-relief from about 700 BC showing servants of King Sennacherib of Assyria (the ancient Near East and Levant) carrying locusts on skewers in preparation for a royal feast.[6] In the New Testament, John the Baptist subsisted on

The Gathering of the Manna, c. 1460–70, oil on panel (likely part of a larger altarpiece), Dutch.

A Turkish pine branch covered with scale insect (*Marchalina hellenica*) excretion, or honeydew. This honeydew is collected by bees and flavours pine honey, a common breakfast condiment in Turkey.

'locusts and wild honey' (Mark 1:6). The Quran mentions that Mohammed ate locusts, too, and received them as gifts from his wives.

The ancient Greeks described grasshoppers and other insect foods. Playwright and poet Aristophanes (*c.* 450–*c.* 388 BC) mentions 'four-winged fowl' (grasshoppers) for sale in the marketplace. In *The Acharnians*, two characters debate whether locusts or thrushes are tastier to eat. The locusts at that time were a food of the poorer classes, while the upper classes preferred cicadas. In *Historia animalium* (The History of Animals), Aristotle writes of cicadas that

> the larva of the cicada on attaining full size in the ground becomes a nymph: then it tastes best, before the husk is broken . . . [as for adults] at first the males are better to eat after copulation than the females, which are then full of white eggs.

The Greek historian Herodotus in the fifth century BC and, later, Diodorus of Sicily described an Ethiopian people they called *Acridophagi*, the locust eaters, who made locusts the central part of their diet. Diodorus, however, disparaged these desert dwellers as sickly and parasite-ridden due to this food.[7]

Of the Romans, the naturalist Pliny the Elder, of the first century AD, noted that a grub called *cossus* (now thought to be the larva of a species of longhorn beetle, *Cerambyx* spp.) was held in high culinary esteem, especially when fattened on flour before cooking.[8]

In China, ancient texts describe large numbers of insects used as food and medicine. In the *Liji* (The Book of Rites) of 475–221 BC, cicadas and bees are listed among fine foods collected and prepared for elites.[9]

Early Modern History: A Shift in the West

Despite the enjoyment of certain insect foods in ancient pre-Western civilizations, by the 'Age of Exploration', opinions about the suitability of insects as food began to shift. Early naturalists, like the Italian Ulisse Aldrovandi, who compiled *De animalibus insectis libri septem* (The Seven Books of Insects, 1602), made special note of the insects eaten by various peoples around the world. Numerous travellers, missionaries and colonial officials recorded the insect-eating practices of the peoples they encountered as interesting facts or curiosities, but not with disgust.

When the Scottish 'privateer' Lionel Wafer wrote *A New Voyage and Description of the Isthmus of America* about his time on the San Blas Islands (1680), he described an 'insect like a snail [*sic*] . . . call'd the "Soldier-Insect"' (actually probably a soldier crab). He finds no need to justify the eating of this 'insect', whose 'Tail especially, is eatable, and is good Food, very well tasted and delicious, like Marrow. We thrust a Skuer through this part and roast a pretty many of them in a row.'[10]

Over the following centuries, however, European observers began to express fascination or repugnance with the insect foods they encountered around the world and often considered these foods of inferior quality and primitive character. By the time William Kirby, often considered the Father of Entomology, and William Spence wrote their *Introduction to Entomology* (published in four volumes between 1815 and 1826), the suitability of insects as human food required an argument. Kirby and Spence wrote of the direct benefits of insects, beginning with their use as 'food for man in which respect they are of more importance than you may have conceived',[11] and they noted that there was little reason but custom that kept them from European tables. Vincent Holt, writing *Why Not Eat Insects?* in 1885, referred to 'a long-existing and deep-rooted public prejudice' and railed against his British compatriots for neglecting insects as food.[12]

Certainly not all Europeans rejected insects. In *Insects as Human Food: A Chapter of the Ecology of Man* (1951), the Israeli entomologist F. S. Bodenheimer described 'relics' of insect eating in the West, such as records from the 1700s and 1800s of various kinds of plant galls (abnormal growths caused by insect infestations) that were appreciated by peoples in Crete, France and the Levant. He also mentioned widespread eating of cockchafer beetles (*Melolontha* spp.) in Europe and noted a number of authors who recorded people in France and Russia consuming various species of grasshoppers into the 1900s.

Contemporary Advocates

A Western bias against insect food meant that it usually did not merit serious attention and was overlooked by scholars. The entomologists who wrote most extensively about insects as food had to do so as a hobby or a side project, separate from their 'serious' scholarly work. *Insects as Human Food*, Bodenheimer's 350-page compendium of food insects from prehistoric to modern times, was not his primary scholarly endeavour.

While a number of historians, anthropologists, entomologists and other scholars (many cited in this book) contributed case studies of insect foods around the world, a few scientists sought to bring the issue to the attention of a broader audience. The entomologist Ronald L. Taylor's 1966 book, *Butterflies in My Stomach; or, Insects in Human Nutrition* (1971), started with a 'random collection of clippings' dealing with insects as human food and the text of an informal talk for his local Rotary Club.[13] Foreshadowing some of today's insect-food proponents, Taylor argued that a coming 'protein crisis' would require the exploration of new sources of food for a hungry planet.[14] Taylor also gave practical advice on obtaining and preparing insects as well as utilizing insects for wilderness survival and medicine.

V. B. Meyer-Rochow, in 1975 a professor of zoology at the University of Western Australia, was an early visionary of the need to investigate insects as human food (where culturally appropriate), as feed for farm animals, and as a commercially viable farming operation, and he saw the potential of breeding insects for greater human food utility.[15] Gene DeFoliart, long-time professor of entomology at the University of Wisconsin–Madison and perhaps the North American most widely associated with insect foods, followed Meyer-Rochow's lead. DeFoliart initially focused on insects' ability to recycle waste materials into protein-rich feed for poultry, fish and livestock. In 1988 he founded the *Food Insects Newsletter*, which compiled information on the nutritional, economic and environmental aspects of insect foods from around the world. The newsletter is still available online.

While DeFoliart conducted serious academic research on several insect food topics, he also enjoyed (and frequently suffered) a level of celebrity as a promoter of these 'novel' and 'exotic' foods. His ideas were given much journalistic attention in the u.s. and he was invited to host and speak at 'bug banquets' across the nation where chefs would do their best to delight attendees with creative bug-based foods.

The 2013 publication of *Edible Insects: Future Prospects for Food and Feed Security* by the Food and Agriculture Organization (FAO) of the United Nations signalled a new era of insect-food study, lending weight and urgency to claims that insects should be considered a part of economic development and sustainable agricultural practices. Overcoming our deep aversion towards insects is important for both cultural understanding and clear consideration of sustainable agricultural systems that will feed the planet into the future.

A Word about Entomophagy and the Western Bias

The words we use to describe people and their foodways reflect our understanding and our attitudes towards them, so let us pause for a moment to consider the word 'entomophagy' and its critics. In English, the term only dates to 1871, when it was used in a book by the British-born American scientist Charles V. Riley (1843–1895), who was one of the leading entomologists of his time. Riley credits a scholar by the name of W. R. Gerard with coining the word.[16] Although still in use, some scholars have begun to avoid it for a number of reasons. First, they argue, the term is ethnocentric. Historically, it was used mostly by non-insect-eating observers (that is, Europeans) to denote an eating habit that was not considered appropriate or 'civilized' in their own cultures. This was a practice used to classify others as 'primitive'.[17]

Another problem is that, like other words ending in '-phagy', 'entomophagy' finds itself in contexts that denote animal behaviour (rather than human behaviour), such as necrophagy (the eating of decaying flesh) or adelphophagy (the eating of one embryo by another *in utero*), the latter of which generally pertains to a practice of certain amphibians.

Beondegi street food, silkworm (*Bombyx mori*) pupae.

The suffix is also associated with strange or pathological eating behaviours, like geophagy (eating of chalk, dirt or clay) or hyalophagy (eating of glass). With these connotations, entomophagy sounds like a harmful medical condition rather than a healthy food practice.

Moreover, people within so-called 'entomophagous' cultures do not think of themselves as 'insect eaters'. They often have no word to indicate 'insect eating' unless such a word was introduced via outside colonial imposition. When I mentioned the topic to a Korean colleague, she said, 'Yuck, people eat insects?!' But then I asked, 'Isn't there a popular dish in Korea called *beondegi*?' Despite my butchered pronunciation, she understood, and her eyes widened. 'Oh yes, silkworm pupae! But I never thought of those as "insects"! I used to eat those all the time, now they are not so common. Only older people still eat them. They are delicious.' My colleague did not associate the English word 'insects' with the specific Korean dish *beondegi*.

Even those people for whom bugs are generally *verboten* sometimes eat them. Although few arthropods are found in German cuisine, some Germans delight in cheeses (*Altenburger Ziegenkäse* and *Milbenkäse*) that have been purposely inoculated with a species of mite (*Tyrophasuc casei*) that colonizes the cheese and gives it a distinct piquant flavour. Similar milk cheeses, processed and flavoured using arthropods, are found elsewhere in Europe. Most famous is Sardinia's *casu marzu* (literally, 'rotten cheese'), a sheep's milk cheese infested with fly (*Piophilia casei*) maggots. These fly larvae break down the fats in the cheese, softening its texture and giving it a pungent, ripe Gorgonzola taste. Although the cheese is served, writhing maggots and all, on a slice of bread, Sardinians still consider casu marzu to be a cheese and not a form of entomophagy. Moreover, the fact that some Italians accept larvae

Casu marzu cheese gets its unique taste from fly (*Piophilia casei*) maggots.

in casu marzu and other cheeses does not mean that they readily eat any other insects.

The case of these European cheeses brings up a related point about *who* we are talking about when we say that people in Western cultures do not generally eat bugs. This is true mostly for the dominant cultures of many European nations, the United States, Canada and Australia. Western cultures, however, are also highly diverse in terms of histories of insect eating. Many indigenous cultures in those areas included insects in their diets and insects are still eaten in some parts of the 'West'. It is also the case that cultures with a long history of insects in their cuisines may now relegate insect foods to a rural or 'traditional' past and not a part of their contemporary, urban, Westernized fare. So 'Western' is a broad but useful generalization that does not fully reflect practices among people in 'the West' or elsewhere.

Everywhere that insects are eaten, there are specific insect food choices with specific names; there are localized norms regarding which insects (and stages of insects) are okay to eat, how they are best prepared and how they should be eaten. The grub called *masinya* is beloved by many Ugandans on the Ssese Islands in Lake Victoria, but they disdain other species of grubs favoured elsewhere in Africa.[18] In the Sahel region, both the Mofu-Gugur in Cameroon and the Hausa of Niger consume grasshoppers, but the species eaten by the former is rejected by the latter and vice versa.

In this way, insect foods are no different to many other foods we eat and the language we use to describe it. Americans eat *beef* (but not *cow*, *cattle* or *Bos taurus*); most prefer steaks or roasts, but not beef tongue or head cheese. Acceptable preparation methods can vary significantly between individuals. Those who like their steak well-done will probably find steak tartare disgusting. It is the same with insect eaters around the world. 'Entomophogy' is misleading; and we need a whole new vocabulary to speak of insect foods.

Emil Schmidt, *A Swarm of Locusts*, pre-1910, chromolithography.

3
Feast or Famine

Yea, even the wasting locusts' swarm,
Which mighty nations dread,
To me nor terror brings nor harm –
For I make of them my bread.
Thomas Pringle (1789–1834), 'Song of the Wild Bushman'

It was a hot and dry summer day in western Missouri, 1875, when the sky suddenly darkened. A farmer's wife looked up from where she was tending her garden, wiped the sweat from her brow, and wondered at the dark cloud on the horizon. Then, with the first pitter-patter of falling insects, she knew, and an icy panic spread through her gut. Soon a blizzard of locusts descended; they landed on every surface, caught in her hair and crawled into her clothes. She gathered her crying children and they ran for shelter, with the locusts crunching beneath their feet. No spot of ground was left uncovered. Over the next few days her terror did not subside. The insects laid waste to a green field of corn in one day, then assaulted the garden and orchard, leaving her family with nothing to harvest. Charity from easterners saved them from starvation that winter. The government sent new seeds, which they planted in the spring, but the devastation came again. The

Grangers versus Hoppers, 1874–75. This *carte-de-visite*, published by the Downing Gallery in Topeka, Kansas, is a cartoon by Kansas artist Henry Worrall showing Kansas farmers (Grangers) battling grasshoppers.

autumn locusts had left their eggs in the ground. In June, a vast army of nymphs would devour every new and tender stem.[1]

Locusts have plagued farmers for millennia. Much like the eighth plague of locusts that befell Egypt in the Bible, they can bring utter devastation. Their visitations are periodic and seemingly random. Awesome in their sheer number and voraciousness, it is no wonder a farmer might see them as God's wrath. Perhaps no insect so clearly represents the utter vulnerability of farmers in the face of nature.

What Is a Locust?

Locusts are species of short-horned grasshoppers within the family Acrididae. Of the some 15,000 Acrididae species, only a dozen can properly be called 'locusts'. A locust species is defined by what it does. Grasshoppers are normally solitary creatures, and when their populations are low-density, they cause minor damage to agriculture. Locusts are grasshopper species that undergo a transformation. Under certain environmental conditions, these grasshopper populations expand, catalysing a 'phase transformation'. That is, the grasshoppers change in size, appearance and behaviour (from solitary creatures to 'gregarious' or highly social). Aggregating into large swarms, these creatures – now properly named 'locusts' – then migrate together in search of food and can cover long distances. Females deposit large numbers of eggs in the soil as they travel. The following season, nymphs emerge and march as a band, eating all in their path. Within a few days, they mature into winged adults, at which point they take flight.

The desert locust (*Schistocerca gregaria*), the probable species of biblical plagues, is perhaps the best-known locust, but there are other widespread species. Records of its swarms extend from ancient Egypt to the present day. During calm periods (called recessions) the desert locust is restricted to desert areas over 16 million square kilometres (6,180,000 sq. mi.) in Africa, the Near East and Southwest Asia. During plagues, however, this species can spread over a vast area of 29 million square kilometres (11,197,000 sq. mi.), affecting parts of sixty countries. FAO monitors locust populations and provides forecasts and warnings to affected countries. The organization's 'Locust Watch' programme tracks the desert locust and a few other species, such as the migratory locust (*Locusta migratorium*) which has a number of subspecies and is found in Africa, Asia, Australia and New Zealand (and previously in Europe). Despite the FAO's surveillance efforts, these episodic but devastating outbreaks are hard to control.

Most farmers worry most about the species of grasshoppers that are perennially problematic. Species such as the Senegalese grasshopper (*Oedaleus senegalensis*) and the African

Desert locust in its solitary versus gregarious forms.

rice grasshopper (*Hierglyphus daganensis*) are considered 'borderline' species, because they are not technically locusts but periodically display swarming behaviours and can cause significant damage to crops.

In a world where most people depend on the production of a few staple grains for their survival, locust swarms continue to cause disaster. They can disrupt several years' worth of crops at a time and contribute to widespread famine. Effective control of the locust outbreaks, mostly with chemical and biological pesticides, is difficult and often limited at best. Even now, researchers still struggle to track and predict locust outbreaks. Historically, however, not everyone dreaded the coming of locusts. Like many agricultural pests, they are devastating only to those who compete with them for food. For the world's foragers and farmers with a variety of crops, the appearance of locusts does not mean starvation and in fact may herald a moment of plenty; a lasting bounty.

Feast

On one hazy afternoon in 1890 during the dry season in Umuofia, Nigeria, the yam harvest was in and Okonkwo and his sons were repairing the earthen walls around the compound. The Igbo village was sleepy and still. Suddenly a thick cloud blocked the sun, casting a deep shadow on the ground. Okonkwo looked up from his work and wondered if it might rain at this unlikely time of year. But then the village erupted in shouts of happiness and joyous activity, 'Locusts are descending!'

First came a fairly small swarm. They were the harbingers sent to survey the land. Then more appeared on the horizon, a slowly moving mass like a boundless sheet of black cloud drifting towards Umuofia. Soon, the insects covered half the sky and the solid mass was broken by tiny eyes of sunlight glinting through the locust bodies like shining stardust. For the villagers, it was a tremendous sight, full of power and beauty.

Such is the description of locusts from Chinua Achebe's classic account of British colonialism and its aftermath in the Niger Delta, *Things Fall Apart*.[2] How different the response from these farmers who, as yet, had not been compelled by the colonial governments to raise grains that the locusts would feast on. No, Achebe shared, these locusts were a rare treat:

> For although locusts had not visited Umuofia for many years, everyone knew by instinct that they were very good to eat . . . many people went out with baskets trying to catch them, but the elders counselled patience till nightfall. And they were right. The locusts settled in the bushes for the night and their wings became wet with dew. Then all Umuofia turned out in spite of the cold harmattan, and everyone filled his bags and pots with

locusts. The next morning they were roasted in clay pots and then spread in the sun until they became dry and brittle. And for many days this rare food was eaten with solid palm oil.[3]

Where insects appear in great numbers, why not make use of such windfall? Indeed, there are many historical accounts of the populations mitigating the destruction of locusts by eating them.

The Year of the Locust

North America is home to some 1,200 species of Acrididae, but has had only one locust species, the Rocky Mountain locust (*Melanoplus spretus*), which was last seen in 1902. Due to widespread eradication efforts and the destruction of the species' grassland habitats, it is now considered extinct. The Rocky Mountain locust outbreak of 1874–5, however, produced the largest locust swarm ever recorded.

In 1874 farmers throughout the central u.s. had already been beleaguered by previous years of widespread drought when vast swarms of the Rocky Mountain locust descended upon parts of northern Colorado, southern Wyoming, Nebraska and the Dakota Territory. As the locusts found new turf, they consumed every green leaf and blade, leaving spring fields looking as bare as winter. Locusts devoured the grasses, then the crops, then turned to the trees, both leaf and bark; there were even accounts of locusts consuming axe handles, cloth, leather stirrups, bridles, gloves and hats. Would-be settlers and farmers were left with nothing. Many new homesteaders in these territories had little choice in the face of such devastation but to give up their lands and return east.

Eggs laid by these locusts in 1874 emerged the following spring, and the nymphs marched on in search of new food. By April 1875 the locusts had spread into the more densely cultivated regions of Minnesota, northwest Iowa and western Missouri.[4] It came to be known as the 'Year of the Locust' in several parts of the North American Midwest.

By July 1875 the locusts had reached their eastern limit and began a return towards the northwest. Aided by southerly winds, they amassed into a huge swarm: an estimated 12.5 trillion insects covered over 318,650 square kilometres (198,000 sq. mi.) – an area larger than the state of California – between Montana and the Rio Grande. One Nebraskan observer testified that a swarm of locusts a mile high passed overhead for five days straight. By telegraphing to neighbouring towns, he was able to estimate that the swarm was 177 kilometres (110 mi.) wide and 2,900 kilometres (1,800 mi.) long.

Mr H. McAllister, of Colorado Springs, reportedly watched the insects come in with the wind:

> In alighting, they circle in myriads about you, beating against everything animate or inanimate, driving in open doors and windows, heaping about your feet and around your buildings, their jaws constantly at work biting and testing all things in seeking what they can devour. In the midst of the incessant buzz and noise that such a fight produces, in the face of the unavoidable destruction everywhere going on, one is bewildered and awed at the collective power of the ravaging host, which calls to mind so forcibly the plagues of Egypt.[5]

Despite the severity of the 1874–5 infestation, locust infestations were certainly not new to Americans and have been recorded in various locations throughout North and

Locust swarm near Satrokala, Madagascar, May 2014.

South America for centuries. Swarms were recorded as early as 1632 in Guatemala; cycles of locust infestations regularly occurred in the western United States throughout the eighteenth and nineteenth centuries; Jesuit missionaries in California reported visitations periodically throughout the 1700s; in the 1800s, outbreaks were reported from as far south as Cordoba, Argentina, to as far north as Manitoba, Canada. Central and South America continue to experience periodic locust outbreaks to this day. The 1874–5 infestation was remarkable in the U.S. not only for its vast range and the economic impact, but for what it taught scientists about the locust and for the national response it garnered.

The young, British-born, self-trained savant Charles Valentine Riley became the state entomologist of Missouri in 1868 – only the third such position to exist in the U.S. at that time. He was on the job when the enormous swarm of locusts spread to the western counties of Missouri. Riley requested insects gathered by farmers from the affected regions to verify that they were all indeed of the same species, now called *Melanoplus spretus* (the Rocky Mountain locust). Riley, who had researched the history of locust outbreaks throughout the Americas, tracked their progress. Based on the history of locust outbreaks and ecology, and his understanding of the locust lifecycle, Riley had correctly predicted the timing of the 1875 outbreak in Missouri, as well as the retreat of the insects later that year when they had reached their eastern limit in western Missouri.

The 1874–5 infestation directly impacted three-quarters of a million people and economic losses were huge in the affected areas. Given the devastation, it was hard for those in the affected regions not to see divine punishment in the plague. Riley, however, advocated strongly that governments respond with charity and relief for affected farmers. When

Missouri's governor called for a day of prayer following the many reports of destruction, Riley responded that surely prayers would be best accompanied by concrete relief efforts. Indeed, the human toll might have been catastrophic without government relief and food donations from eastern states.

Riley was at the forefront of helping governments and farmers understand the insect and how to manage the infestation. He urged the u.s. Congress to establish an Entomological Commission to study this insect and other agricultural pests, which they did in 1876 and named Riley chief entomologist. With increased visibility, resources and experience, Riley proposed a number of practical solutions for combating outbreaks, including the digging of trenches to trap marching nymphs and properly timed tilling to bury the eggs deep enough so they would not be able to hatch. One of Riley's solutions for locust control seemed far-fetched but was widely reported in the newspapers of the time: why not *eat* the locusts?

Locusts for Dinner?

Charles V. Riley knew that locusts of the Old World were eaten extensively, that they were usually stripped of their wings and legs, and then either boiled, roasted, fried, smoked, stewed, broiled or grilled, and relished by various peoples across the Middle East and Africa. He knew that various indigenous peoples of North America consumed 'New World' grasshoppers, very probably the same *M. spretus* – or a closely related species – that was ravaging the American West. He also observed that other animals ate the grasshoppers eagerly and with no ill effect. The locust invasion in the Mississippi Valley gave Riley an opportunity to fulfil a long-desired opportunity to test the use of the species as food. He did so for more than mere curiosity's sake; for some people in the region were on the verge of starvation.

Riley reports in his book *The Locust Plague in the United States* (1877) that he consumed grasshoppers whenever the occasion presented itself, prepared in a variety of ways, and always found them palatable. He noted that they require little preparation, beyond cooking and adding some seasoning.[6]

He sought the opinions of others and staged dinners so that they might see for themselves, although his efforts were not always warmly greeted. He recounts his first attempt, which was made at a hotel in Warrensburg, Missouri, where he had no luck enlisting the kitchen staff in assisting him. Left to his own talents, and with 'the interest and aid of a brother naturalist and two intelligent ladies', he prepared a number of dishes. As a savoury and pleasant odour went up from the cooking dishes,

> The expression of horror and disgust gradually vanished from the faces of the curious lookers on . . . at last, the head cook, – a stout and jolly negress – took part in the operations . . . The soup soon vanished and banished silly prejudice; then cakes with batter enough to hold the locusts together disappeared, and were pronounced good; then baked locusts with or without condiments; and when the meal was completed with dessert of baked locusts and honey *à la* John the Baptist, the opinion was unanimous that the distinguished prophet no longer deserved our sympathy, and that he had not fared badly on his diet in the wilderness.[7]

The Rocky Mountain locust made appearances in the years following 1875 but never in such numbers and with such destructiveness. The continued settlement of the American West and the introduction of plough agriculture and cattle grazing dramatically altered the ecosystem of the West's river valleys (the Rocky Mountain grasshopper's habitat) and eventually resulted in the extinction of the locust.[8] What remains are memories of its ravages, which so shaped the West, the pioneer experience and the character of the u.s., both politically and socially.[9]

Riley's locust dinners were largely meant to be spectacles. Serving them to members of the u.s. Congress brought attention to the plight of Western farmers and dramatized his feeling that insect eating might alleviate much of the suffering brought about by the insects; however, he knew that eating the locusts would probably not take hold. Despite Riley's own positive experiences, as well as those of others, he admitted that

> our western farmers who occasionally suffer from them [locusts] will not easily be brought to a due appreciation of them for this purpose. Prejudiced

Map of North America showing native area of Rocky Mountain locust and extent of its range, by Charles Valentine Riley, 1877.

against them, fighting to overcome them, killing them in large quantities, until the stench from their decomposing bodies becomes at times most offensive – they find little that is attractive in the pests. For these reasons, as long as other food is attainable, the locust will be apt to be rejected by most persons.[10]

Indeed, they have been.

Eating Agricultural Pests

Riley was certainly not the first person to suggest eating locusts as agricultural pest control. Immanuel Kant wrote that German political theorist Ludolph Hugo took locusts that were plaguing Germany in 1693 and cooked them in what is traditionally a crayfish preparation, preserving them with vinegar and pepper. He then treated the Council of Frankfurt, who had been summoned to discuss the problem, to this locust dish.[11] His idea was heeded about as well as Riley's in 1877.

The idea of eating insects as pest control has not been rejected in other parts of the world. When an outbreak of Bombay locusts (*Patanga succincta* L.) attacked maize fields in Thailand and remained uncontrolled even after spraying, the Thai government launched a campaign to promote the eating of *Patanga*. Though many insects are eaten by the Thai, this species was not a well-known edible. The campaign ran from 1978 to 1981 and many approaches to preparing the species were tried. Deep-fried *Patanga* locust is now one of the most popular edible insects in Thailand despite the fact that the species is no longer a major pest for farmers. In fact, some farmers raise maize to feed *Patanga*, which are in high demand and sell for a high price.[12]

In southern Mexico, grasshoppers and other insects have been a prominent part of the cuisine from the times prior to the colonization of indigenous peoples up to the present. Grasshoppers, called *chapulines*, are particularly popular in the state of Oaxaca, where large baskets heaped high with the spiced insects can be found on many street corners and in multiple marketplaces. These grasshoppers are collected from fields, cleaned, prepared and sold in markets. They are a significant source of protein for the local people and a source of income for those who sell them.[13]

An agricultural study in the neighbouring Mexican state of Puebla, where chapulines are also popular, compared the traditional manual harvesting of grasshoppers (*Sphenarium purpurascens*) in alfalfa fields to the use of chemical pesticides for pest control. Hand harvesting was determined to be equally effective at managing the agricultural pest, thus reducing expenditure on pesticides as well as soil and water contamination, while having the added benefit of producing a profitable food item.[14]

Feast or Famine?

In Chinua Achebe's novel, the initially celebrated locusts are a metaphor for another kind of invasion, that of Europeans and missionaries in Africa, which would eventually be as destructive as locusts became to Africa's people and cultures. Anthropologist Hugh Raffles provides a contemporary cautionary tale from Niger illustrating some of the continuing contradictions surrounding grasshoppers.

As Raffles relates, for people of the Sahel region of Africa (a belt of land that stretches from the Atlantic Ocean to the Red Sea), grasshoppers have been both a source of sustenance

Chapulines for sale on the street, Oaxaca, Mexico.

and a source of famine, whenever a plague of desert locusts occasionally appears. More troubling, however, is the chronic existence of other borderline grasshopper species that can wreak havoc on crops even at lower population densities. The various grasshopper species of the Sahel region are collectively referred to as *les criquets* in French, or *houara* in the native Hausa language. The Hausa have long made use of houara in their diets. They became agricultural pests only after the colonial governments attempted to impose groundnut and millet farming on the region. Today, only wealthy farmers can afford pesticides against grasshoppers, and those pesticides have been terribly ineffective in the dramatic cases of periodic locust plagues that have visited the Sahel region.[15]

Village women collect *houara* to support otherwise meagre resources. Today, it is not only the Hausa who appreciate grasshoppers, but the relatively well-off urbanites who enjoy *les criquets* as a 'special food', a snack bought in the open markets as a treat that one occasionally brings home to eat with friends and family. There is a brisk trade in *houara*. Raffles has followed the trade route and accompanied village women collecting the hourara under shrubs, snapping their hind legs and throwing them into cotton bags. In September, when the grasshoppers abound, collection is easy, but during the low season in January, the women must hunt for them. There are some years when the *houara* supply is bountiful and women can earn enough to buy a cow and have plenty of grasshoppers to eat; but there are years when none come at all.

Fara grasshopper snacks for sale in Jalingo, Nigeria.

Hausa woman selling peanuts at a street market in Nigeria.

Even in low seasons when scarcity drives up the price in the market, the houara garner these women a pittance. Village women sell their catch to a trader who in turn sells to the kingpin of the regional market. From the regional trader, *les criquets* will eventually end up with the market-stall retailer. With each trading stage the price is marked up and all the middlemen (who are indeed all men) each get their cut. The village women, however, must take what they can get for their meagre catch since they have no other means to earn cash to buy clothes, supplies and food for their families. The food they wind up purchasing with their money will most probably be of greater volume but lesser nutritional quality than the grasshoppers they caught.[16]

Locust plagues continue to wreck havoc on vast regions of Africa, the Middle East and parts of Asia, provoking famine and periodically threatening the livelihood of one-tenth of humanity. Climate change and global warming have created conditions for larger and more damaging locust swarms into the future. Because widespread chemical spraying is now a primary form of defence, locusts in many places are no longer safe to eat.

Painting by Long Jack Phillipus Tjakamarra (*c.* 1932–2020), a Ngalia/ Warlpiri artist of his country in the desert near Papunya Central Australia, date unknown.

4
Rustling Up Some Grub(s) around the World

Most edible insects are collected from the wild and are only seasonally available. Traditional cultures developed remarkable methods for locating, collecting and preparing insects. Some brief examples from around the world provide only the most cursory introduction to insect food procurement and gastronomy past and present.

Australia

Insects were historically important foods of the various indigenous people of Australia, who flourished in even the harshest arid environments. Writing in 1896, the Australian anthropologist and physiologist E. C. Stirling noted of the central Australian indigenous people that 'to mention the names of all [the animals] that are eaten would be largely to recapitulate the zoology of the district.'[1] Yet detailed knowledge about the insect foods of Aboriginal Australians is limited to a few species: the witchetty grubs (*Endoxyla leucomochla*), bogong moths (*Agrotis infusa*), honeypot ants (*Melophorus* spp.) and 'sugarbag' bees (for example, *Tetragonula carbonaria*).

Witchetty grubs are larvae of a cossid wood moth that feeds on the root sap of the witchetty bush (although *witchetty* is often used generically for other edible grubs across Australia). In central Australia, the witchetty grub was once the preferred food out of 25 uniquely named edible insect larvae.[2] Women and children dug up the roots of the bush to find the grubs, which can be eaten raw, cooked in hot ashes or skewered and roasted. When cooked, the skin becomes crispy while the insides remain creamy. The taste has been deliciously described as 'nut-flavored scrambled eggs and mild mozzarella, wrapped in a phyllo dough pastry'.[3] These grubs are a hearty bite too. They reach about 7 centimetres (2¾ in.) long and are rich in fat and protein, with 245 calories per 100 grams (3½ oz).

The bogong moth was once an important food for numerous Aboriginal peoples of the Australian Alps. Although there are many edible butterfly and moth species, most are consumed at the caterpillar stage. The Aboriginal Australians of Mount Bogong region, however, were unusual in their consumption of adult moths. During the hot season, the

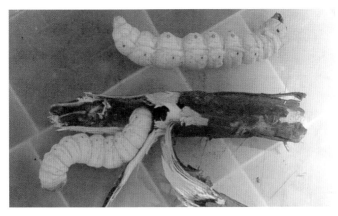

Witchetty grubs (*Endoxyla leuchmochla*).

Bogong moths (*Agrotis infusa*) in estivation in the High Country, Victoria, Australia.

moths enter a period of dormancy, called aestivation, during which they congregate on mountain cave walls and in crevices and are easy to collect. Cooked in sand and hot ash to burn off the wings and legs, the roasted bodies, which are up to 60 per cent fat, could be consumed plain or made into pastes and cakes.

Honeypot ants are found in arid environments around the world, where they are often rare sources of sweetness. They are called honeypot (or honey) ants because certain special-ized members of the colony, called repletes, use their abdomens to store a sweet sap that they share with other members when food is scarce. People relish the large sweet ants wherever they are found, but they are not easy to harvest. To access their below-ground nests, one must dig deep shafts parallel to the ants' nest – sometimes up to 2 metres (6½ ft) deep – and then tunnel into the side to reach the gallery where the ants reside. The ants are eaten by holding the head and biting into their fat belly.

Beyond insects' many functional uses as food, medicine, bait, adhesives, adornment and toys, many are also 'cultural

Honeypot ants (*Melophorus* spp.) with sweet abdomens.

keystone species'; that is, they are important for Aboriginal Australians' cultural identity. These keystone species are food items but are also celebrated in creation stories, ceremonial songs and artistic designs, as well as in personal and place names.[4] Papunya, a small community in Australia's Northern Territory that gave birth to the famous Papunya Tula art movement of the Western Desert, is an example. 'Papunya Tula' means 'Honey Ant Dreaming', which is a creation story. This dreaming belongs to the various tribes who live in that region and references the honeypot ants and the land. The art movement began in the 1970s when village elders created the *Honey Ant Mural* on the side of a school. The 'dot and circle' style gave birth to a revolutionary art movement that flourishes yet today.[5]

As this example illustrates, indigenous names, ceremonies and mythology related to insects intertwine complex eco-logical and social knowledge, much of which has been lost due to displacement and destruction of Aboriginal peoples. Aboriginal communities today continue to fight to retain their cultures and establish rights. Although witchetty grubs and honeypot ants are featured in outback tourism and in trendy restaurants featuring bush tucker and native foods, much indigenous knowledge about these foods and their environment has yet to be recognized.

Brazil

Brazil is not particularly well known for insect fare. Although many indigenous Amazonian peoples consume insects, few insects are consumed outside those communities. The one exception is *tanajura* or *içá*, a species of leaf-cutter ant (*Atta cephalotes*) which is a seasonal treat enjoyed in many rural areas. For a brief time after spring rains, the winged females emerge from large earthen nests to establish new colonies. Aficionados brave the biting soldier ants to collect the tanajuras from the ground, usually by picking them up swiftly by the wings and putting them into buckets. In the kitchen, they are prepared by washing and then pinching off the legs, head and wings. The desired abdomen is then fried in lard or butter. Once they are crispy and fully cooked, dried manioc meal and other ingredients are added to make a version of the popular Brazilian dish *farofa*.

China

The record of insects for food and medicine dates back thousands of years in China. Entomologists have identified over 178 edible insect species in China, with most belonging to three orders: butterfly and moth (Lepidoptera); beetle (Coleoptera); and bee, wasp and ant (Hymenoptera). Although dozens of edible species are common in markets and restaurants throughout China today, insect-eating practices are regionally distinct. While ants and honeybees are eaten widely, silk moth pupae were traditionally associated with Jiangsu and Zhejiang provinces, while the giant water beetle was limited to Guangdong Province.

Herodutus' dictum 'Let food be thy medicine and medicine be thy food' well expresses a principle of traditional Chinese medicine. The black ant (*Polyrhachis vicina* Roger) is considered China's most important edible insect,[6] although it is perhaps better thought of as a nutritional supplement or health food than culinary delight. A quick Internet search turns up numerous companies marketing Chinese 'mountain black ant' powder and tonic for benefits as diverse as sexual dysfunction, hair loss, athletic endurance and improved concentration. The consumption of black ants for their health-giving properties is a long-lived practice.[7] In the classic Chinese medical reference book the *Compendium of Materia Medica*, Li Shizhen (1518–1593) indicated that black ants 'enrich the *qi*, beautify skin, delay ageing and restore kidney energy'. Modern scientific evidence provides some explanations for its potential efficacy. Some *Polyrhachis* species produce formic acid, an antibiotic, and others have significant anti-inflammatory properties. Recent chemical analyses show that *P. vicina* ants are indeed a health food, rich in amino acids and minerals.[8]

Manchurian, or golden, scorpions (*Mesobuthus martensii*) have also been important in traditional Chinese medicine. They were once caught in the wild but are now mostly farmed and used as a snack food in the south of China. At the popular night markets, scorpions are among the myriad offerings that are likely to catch a tourist's eye. Displayed still squirming

Cooking black ants for wine tonic, Zhaoxing Dong Village, Guizhou Province, China.

on their skewers, they are served after a quick fry in hot oil. Although their tails look formidable, their toxin is neutralized upon exposure to heat. The taste is described as similar to soft-shelled crab.

India

Eating insects is an age-old tradition for many Adivasi, original peoples of India, and the practice remains common in the northeastern states.[9] A study in Nagaland, for instance, found

Scorpions and other culinary delights at Wangfujing in Beijing.
Nests of the hornet *Vespa mandarina* for sale in northeast India.

that over a hundred insect species, representing 32 families and nine orders, play an important alimentary role in the region. Dragonflies, grasshoppers, locusts, crickets, stink bugs, ant larvae, and grubs of all sorts of bees and wasps are among the insects utilized, although Naga of different tribes vary in their preferred insects and preparation techniques. Hornet larvae (*Vespa mandarina*) are also harvested from inside their combs. Although bee, wasp and hornet grubs can be eaten raw, most insects are boiled, roasted or fried in oil along with local spices such garlic, ginger, fermented bamboo shoot and powdered sumac. The Nagas are farmers and can harvest large numbers of grasshoppers and katydids from their fields to be sundried or smoked and saved for year-round use.[10]

Japan

Insect consumption in Japan today is rare and largely confined to the mountainous central region, where some rural villagers hunt, harvest and eat wasp larvae and pupae. People relish the brood of several species of wasp (*Vespula* spp.) as an autumnal delicacy called *hachinoko*, but the wasps' underground nests are hard to locate and must be harvested with great skill to avoid being stung.[11]

They have developed an ingenious method for finding a nest, an activity called 'chasing' that involves whole families and friends. First, at the appropriate time of year, a chaser leaves a pungent piece of skewered meat in the forest as bait. When a worker wasp finds the bait, the chaser offers it a tiny wasp-sized meatball that has a small ribbon flag attached. If the wasp accepts the offer, it will take the tagged meatball back to the nest. The chase then ensues, with the chaser and helpers trailing behind the flagged wasp, scrabbling up rocks and climbing trees, to follow its path to the nest. If they locate the entrance of the nest, the wasps inside must be sedated with smoke. Then, skilled harvesters wear protective clothing to dig out and remove the entire nest.

If the nest is immature, it may be put into a special house made for caring and feeding the brood until ready for harvest.

Once the nest is ready, it is brought into the home and family members carefully remove the larvae and pupae one by one, a time-consuming process. The brood is often prepared by boiling it with soy sauce or frying it, and then mixing it with rice. Hachinoko is celebrated at annual wasp festivals during the harvest season.

Another insect speciality, from Nagano Prefecture, dates from the Edo period (1603–1868). At the upper reaches of the Tenryugawa River, fishermen collect the aquatic larvae of several insect species of the orders Megaloptera and Tricoptera (caddisfly). Known collectively as *zazamushi*, the small larvae live under rocks at the bottom of the river. When the water is low, between December and February, fishermen catch the *zazamushi* in nets hung from a bamboo structure. After washing in warm water they are often prepared with soy sauce and sugar (*tsukudani*).

Zazamushi (caddisfly larvae) tsukudani.

A *hebo* (wasp) hunter attracts a worker wasp with a flagged bit of meat, Gifu Prefecture, central Japan.

Hachinoko (wasp brood) for sale in Japan.

Mexico

In the western hemisphere, Mexico is undoubtedly the epicentre of insect cuisine. The escamoles I relish are just one of as many as 549 insect species traditionally enjoyed by rural peoples throughout Mexico. Insect foods have a deep and rich cultural history stretching back to pre-Hispanic times. Although some of these traditions disappeared or were discouraged under years of colonial influence, many rural people and indigenous groups continued to collect and use insects as an important part of their diet and culture. Traditional knowledge of insect foods persisted in rural communities where peasant farmers made use of the native foods, including insects, to supplement their diets. But these culinary resources are not limited to those with restricted resources – many insect foods are enjoyed by all social classes. In Oaxaca State, researchers found that at least 78 species of insects are eaten. They were utilized as much by those living in the poorest, most arid regions as those living on the coast with access to the sea, rivers and better soil.[12]

Many of these native foods are enjoyed across social classes. Jumil bugs, for instance, are a type of stink bug (*Euschistus taxcoensis*) native to the states of Guerrero and Morelos. Jumiles have their own holiday, Holy Jumil, on 1 November. Residents of the city of Taxco continue a celebration initiated by the Aztecs, who made annual pilgrimages to collect the bug on the Cerro del Huixteco, a mountain north of the city, and constructed a temple there in its honour. Jumiles are believed to have analgesic and anaesthetic properties. They may be eaten raw but are also ground with tomatillos and peppers to make a salsa and are sometimes eaten toasted on tacos. They have a unique sweet-bitter flavour that some consider 'medicinal', in part due to their high iodine content.

Maguey caterpillars prepared for tacos, Oaxaca, Mexico.

Some of the most widely appreciated Mexican insect foods are red or white maguey worms which are actually caterpillars. Both are the 'worms' sometimes placed in bottles of mezcal, but more often they are simply fried up as a snack. The 'red worms', also called *chinicuiles* or *gusano rojo*, are the caterpillars of the moth *Comadia redtenbacheri*, which feeds on succulent agave leaves. The *chinicuiles* are used to make *sal de gusano* (worm salt), which traditionally accompanies lime and a shot of mezcal. White maguey worms, or *meocuiles*, are the caterpillars of the butterfly *Acentrocneme hesperiaris*. These caterpillars are collected mostly in northeastern areas of Tlaxcala and Hidalgo.

Thailand

Insects are a significant food item in Thailand. Traditionally, insect eating was associated with ethnic groups in the northern and northeastern regions, but today numerous insect foods can be found throughout the country and are enjoyed widely among the population. As many as two hundred species of insects (spiders and scorpions) are consumed in Thailand. Most of these are still collected in the wild, but a few, such as crickets and palm weevils, are raised for the nation's thriving insect farming industry.

Some of the traditional insect foods were recorded in the 1930s by the English naturalist William. S. Bristowe, who was impressed by Thai and ethnic Lao peoples' skilful means of obtaining them.[13]

For instance, weaver ants (*Oecophylla smaragdina*) build thick nests the size of a tennis ball or football. People collect the ant pupae from the nests by submerging them in water or by harvesting the nest with a pole and basket.

Weaver ant (*Oecophylla smaragdina*) nest made of leaves and larval silk.

Cicadas are another traditional item that is cleverly collected. Bristowe recorded that cicada hunters would gather around a fire at night and rapidly clap bamboo sticks together to produce a sound which mimicked the male mating call. In response, female cicadas would descend in large numbers for easy collection.

Among the more interesting delicacies consumed in Thailand, and throughout Southeast Asia, is the giant water bug, *Lethocerus indicus*, which resembles a cockroach and can reach 5–7.6 centimetres (2–3 in.) in length. The bugs are eaten plain or used in sauces. The larger, meatier, female of the species is often steamed or fried. To eat them, one first pulls off the hard outer wings and splits the head from the abdomen.

Giant water bugs (*Lethocerus indicus*).

Then the meat can be sucked out of both parts. The smaller male of the species is prized for the stronger taste it has thanks to the pheromones it produces to attract females. Their taste is variously described as similar to Gorgonzola cheese, liquorice or tart apple dipped in salt.

The United States

Edible insects are fewer in northern America (north of Mexico) than in tropical regions. Before European colonization, several insects were important for the Native Americans in the western and southwestern regions. The Kutzadika'a, literally 'fly eaters', were a small group of hunter-gatherers who lived in the Mono Basin near the saline Mono Lake. The Kutzadika'a collected shore fly (*Ephydra hians*) pupae in the shallow waters and on the shores of the lake.

Adult shore flies lay eggs in the water. When the eggs hatch, the larvae attach themselves to rocks and often to each other to form large, floating mats. As the pupae form, they detach themselves from the mass and start to move towards shore, often helped along by wind and waves, thus washing up in long windrows at the shore. For those who lived near the salt lakes, the pupae, or *kutsavi*, could be gathered in huge quantities, eaten without further preparation or stored for months. One observer, J. Ross Brown, adventurer and government agent, who travelled to Mono Lake in September 1865, wrote:

> Deposits of worms [*sic*] about two feet high by three or four in thickness, extended like a vast rim around the shores of the lake . . . The Mono Indians derive from it a fruitful source of subsistence. By drying them in the sun and mixing them with acorns, berries, grass-seeds and other articles of food . . . they make a conglomerate called *cuchaba* . . . a kind of bread . . . It is considered a delicacy to fry them in their own grease. When properly prepared by a skillful cook they resemble pork 'cracklings' . . . There is no danger of starvation on the shore of the Mono. The inhabitants may be snowed in, flooded out or cut off by aboriginal hordes, but they can always rely upon the beach for fat meat.[14]

No one harvests *kutsavi* now. European-American mining and settlement of the basin eventually forced the Kutzadika'a from the land. Today a small group of descendants are fighting to obtain federal recognition of their tribe.

Zimbabwe

Insect consumption is still widespread in many African countries. It is most common in the Democratic Republic of the Congo, the Central African Republic, Cameroon, Uganda, Zambia, Zimbabwe, Nigeria and South Africa. In Zimbabwe, the most popular insect food is the mopane worm. The collection and trade of mopane worms has become a multimillion-dollar industry in Zimbabwe, Botswana and South Africa.

The mopane 'worm' is the caterpillar of the emperor moth (*Gonimbrasia belina*), which feeds mostly on mopane trees and is found across southern Africa. The mature caterpillars are very large, 8–10 centimetres (3–4 in.), long and must be picked off trees. Harvesting mopane caterpillars is typically the job of women and youths, while men often work trading the insects. A skilled picker working on a tree with an average infestation can pick 18 kilograms (40 lb) per hour. They are prepared by pinching one end of the worm and squeezing it to expel the green innards. Then they are boiled in salty water and laid out to sun-dry. They can also be smoked,

Mopane (*Gonimbrasia belina*) caterpillars on tree.

Dried mopanes at market.

pickled or fried. Dried and bagged, these fetch a good price in the marketplaces and thus can be a good source of income for rural households.

Because mopane worms offer nutrition and livelihood for the rural poor throughout much of Africa, they are in high demand. Attempts at quick harvest can tear branches and damage the trees, which are valuable as firewood, construction material and medicine. Increasing demand for all of these these products, coupled with climate change, could rapidly deplete mopane woodlands unless sustainable management practices are implemented.[15]

Insect Gastronomy

The few short examples given here only hint at the diverse nutritional and medicinal benefits of insects and the culinary opportunities they provide. Far from being an emergency food of last resort, insects are appreciated around the world for their nutritive and flavour characteristics. The indigenous people and rural populations who have traditionally utilized these resources possess important knowledge of insect ecology, life cycle, means of collection and rearing, as well as preparation and use. Retaining and reclaiming this knowledge depends on indigenous food sovereignty and respect for their cultural heritage.

Epicurean readers will perhaps lament that most edible insects encountered in urban markets today are prepared simply; they are eaten raw or are boiled, baked or fried. This homogenization of insect cuisine likely reflects the commercial and market worlds into which insect foods have entered, and is not an accurate representation of traditional cookery. After all, dried and fried insects are an expedient and filling food, an excellent street food or snack, even if they end up tasting much like the oil in which they are fried.

For counterpoint, I end with a mysterious and provocative account recorded by W. S. Bristowe on his travels in Thailand. He describes one particularly elaborate dish prepared by forest people near Suphan. The recipe starts with the evisceration of a long-tailed kharang (genus *Presbytis*) monkey whose body is stuffed with lime leaves and other herbs and sewn shut. The full carcass is then completely covered with a paste of clay made from the interior of a termite mound. The enclosed carcass is hung from the branch of a tree with a dish placed below it. The juice that drops into it is called 'monkey sauce' and is highly regarded. He continues,

After the monkey has been hanging a week or two . . .
maggots begin to fall into the dish, and . . . When no
more fall the remaining shell is cut open and two to
three special big maggots of a different kind are found
inside. Judging by the description . . . this is a beetle
larva. As many coconuts as there are larvae are collected
and heated in their shells, a hole is bored into the top
and, when the liquid is cool, one larva is introduced into
each. The hole is now closed with termite paste, the coconut is swathed with cloth and this in turn is enclosed in
termite paste. For about three weeks this 'mummy' is
stored away and then, when it is split open, a white grub
'the size of a tangerine orange' is found practically filling the interior of the coconut. How great a delicacy
this is can be gathered from the fact that to buy *one*
would cost . . . a fortune to these country folk.[16]

Sadly, Bristowe was unable to identify the species or to provide other important details for this complex gastronomic
tale. While this case is surely exceptional, it illustrates that
some traditional insect preparations required extensive entomological knowledge and skill, much of which has been lost.
Moreover, the current popularity of insects in urban Thailand
takes a form (frying) that was not part of the traditional cuisine and does not well represent traditional uses or even their
gastronomic potential.[17]

Silkworm cocoons being processed, Vietnam.

5
Rearing Mini-livestock

An ancient Chinese legend says that Empress Xi Ling-shi, wife of the Yellow Emperor, accidentally discovered silk while sipping tea under a mulberry tree. A cocoon fell into her teacup and it began to unravel. Enamoured of its glistening fibre, the empress developed sericulture, the rearing of silkworms for the production of silk. If this legend were complete, however, it would tell us that once the silk fibre was removed, the empress took the spent and steamed pupa from her teacup, popped it in her mouth and declared it a tasty and nutritious bite.

Silk can be produced from the cocoons of several insects, but most comes from *Bombyx mori*, the domestic silk moth. While many species of insects are raised in captivity, silk moths carry the distinction of being one of only three insect species that humans have ever fully domesticated; the other two species are the honeybee and cochineal.

Domestication is the lengthy process of adapting wild species of plants and animals for human use and benefit. Selective breeding produces offspring with desired characteristics. Over thousands of years in China, silk producers selected moths for larger cocoon size, faster growth and development and better survival in the crowded conditions of captivity. Controlling a wild species' environment is the first stage in the process of domestication. The common house cricket (*Acheta domesticus*) can be farmed (or ranched, if you will), but these captive populations of crickets do not differ considerably from their wild counterparts. Increasing human control and intervention into the reproductive cycle results in further domestication. The *Bombyx mori* moth, as a fully domesticated species, is very different from closely related wild moth species (for example, *B. mandarina*). *B. mori* has lost the ability to fly and is wholly dependent on humans for its survival.[1]

Why humans have not domesticated more insects is a complex question, but most insect species are simply not suitable for domestication.[2] Species amenable to domestication must be able to reproduce easily in captivity and have a high growth rate so that the benefit of keeping them outweighs the cost of their maintenance. Very few animal species possess these characteristics – only fourteen mammals. The three domesticated insect species are valuable more for their products than for the consumption of the insect itself, but their alimentary uses should not be overlooked.

Silkworm Pupae

The earliest evidence of silk production is dated to over 8,500 years ago, in Jiahu, Henan Province, China, where archaeologists have found bone needles, rudimentary weaving tools and biomolecular evidence of silk in excavated tombs.[3] The silk moth feeds almost exclusively on the leaves of the mulberry tree, so sericulture entails the dual enterprise of cultivating mulberry trees and raising the silkworms.

After the eggs hatch, silkworms (moth larvae) must be fed a continual diet of chopped fresh mulberry leaves. Silkworms

Silkworm processing, print from *Everyday Life in Old China*, pre-1927, artist unknown.

feed until they enter the pupal stage, at which time they begin to spin their puffy white cocoons from long silk protein filaments. If the pupa is allowed to emerge from the cocoon, the precious thread is damaged. Thus producers drop the mature cocoons into hot water to loosen the fibres, which is then pulled and wound onto a spool. In this process the pupae inside the cocoons are cooked and left behind.

Traditionally, silk production in China was women's work. While men cared for the mulberry trees, women tended to the cocoons, processed them and spun the silk threads. The perk of this highly skilled labour was the ever-present snack of silkworm pupae. In 1947 W. E. Hoffman, an American economic entomologist working at Lingnan University in Canton, China, explained that:

> In reeling the cocoons are dropped into very hot water and the reeling girls have a plentiful supply of freshly cooked food before them all day long. They seem to eat off and on all day long since they work rapidly for long

hours at a stretch, and the cooked morsels are constantly before them. One gets a pleasant odour of food being cooked, when passing through a reeling factory.[4]

It takes 2,000–3,000 cocoons to make 450 grams (1 lb) of silk, so silkworm pupae are an abundant by-product of silk production and can be sold at foodstalls. Bodenheimer reported that silkworm production in rural China was a seasonal endeavour, but people processed the pupae for year-round use:

> The cocoons of silkworms cropped in the spring are preserved by baking or by pickling them with common salt . . . The pupae from either the baked cocoons or from the salted cocoons are then dried in the sun and preserved as food for the rest of the year. Pupae from the baked cocoons are more delicious and are liked the most. For eating the pupae are first softened in water and then fried either with chicken eggs in the form of omelette or simply fried with onion and sauce. It is used as a dish in the ordinary meal or on occasions when guests are invited.[5]

Today, silkworm pupae are found in stores and menus in China (fried in oil or barbequed on skewers) and in Vietnam (fried and prepared as various dishes). In Korea, they became especially important as a food source during times of war. Called *beondegi* (literally, 'pupae'), they are still boiled, seasoned and sold as street food. In Japan, silkworm pupae are usually served as a *tsukudani*, cooked in a sweet-and-sour sauce made with soy sauce and sugar.

Opinions differ wildly on the taste of silkworm pupae. They have been described as fishy, musty, earthy, nutty, like

Silkworm pupae, mealworms, lime and ground peanut in a curried soup.

raw meat and like potato. Others say they taste very mild. In her book of essays *Think I'll Go Eat a Worm* (2019), Amy Wright described the canned version she tried as 'bite-sized turkey livers steeped in formaldehyde'. Depending on the preparation, the outside may be crunchy or chewy. In the creamed and curried soup pictured in this chapter, they were chewy and had a 'gamey' taste.

Honeybee Brood

Of some 20,000 species of bees, only eleven extant species worldwide are honeybees, and only two – the western honeybee (*Apis mellifera*) and the eastern honeybee (*Apis cerana*) – are commonly considered to be domesticated. The western honeybee is by far the most common in commercial apiculture (beekeeping) worldwide and is the most economically important species today for its role as a crop pollinator and for its many products (honey, wax, propolis, royal jelly).

Some biologists, however, debate whether *Apis mellifera* is a fully domesticated or simply a managed species. Beekeeping does not require domestication. At the simplest level, beekeepers create spaces and conditions conducive to a bee colony in a location that will facilitate honey collection. The keeping of stingless bees (*Melipona* spp), or meliponiculture, dates to the Mayan civilization and is still practised in Central and South America, as well as Australia. At the other end of the domestication scale are mass production and selective bee-breeding programmes, of which *Apis mellifera* has been the focus. Unlike the silk moth, *A. mellifera* is still able to breed with wild relatives and they frequently go feral (such that swarms are often to be found where they are unwanted).[6]

Although we usually only think of honey, when considering bees as food, cultures from western North America, South America, Asia and Africa have made culinary use of certain bee (and wasp) species from larva to adult as we saw from examples in India and Japan.

Today, some researchers have advocated eating honeybee brood as a sustainable protein source that would also benefit bee populations in the U.S., which have been declining in part due to the Varroa mites that attack the combs. By thinning the drone (sterile male) combs, the apiarist can control the mite infestations and generate a high-protein food source; the ratio and quality of protein in honeybee brood is similar to beef.[7] Bee larvae and pupae are said to have a nutty flavour when cooked and dried and are considered a delicacy in many countries.

Despite numerous requests to my local beekeeping association, I have yet to find anyone who will share their brood with me, but one apiarist described how she harvested and eats brood herself. Given the public's general affection for honeybees, relative to other insects, perhaps honeybee brood could serve as a gateway insect food for even the most sceptical Western consumers.

Cochineal

Cochineal (*Dactylopius coccus*) is a scale insect that feeds on prickly pear cactus. It is the source of carmine, a red dye used in foods, cosmetics and textiles. Native to Central and South America, cochineal has been harvested and used in Mexico and Peru since pre-Hispanic times and was one of the most economically important global trade items of the 1600s. More vibrant than the dyes available in Europe at the time, cochineal provided the red of the British Army redcoats. Although production of carmine declined in the 1800s due to the invention of synthetic substitutes, production surged again in the 1900s as consumers sought natural dyes.

Traditionally, 'cochineal scale' was scraped off the cactus plants *in situ*. Today, cochineal producers collect the cactus leaves that cochineal live on and hang them in a greenhouse. When the cochineal are ready to harvest, they are scraped off the leaves. After harvest, the insects are dried and crushed into the powder that becomes a vibrant dye, yielding a wide range of pink and red hues when mixed with water. It takes about 70,000 insects to make just 450 grams (1 lb) of dye. Today's largest producers are Peru, Mexico and the Canary Islands.

Carmine is a remarkably bright and stable natural colourant found in a large number of food and beverage products. It can cause allergic reactions in a small number of people but is not known to be harmful to health or carcinogenic like

Carmine of cochineal smeared on a woman's hand used for dying thread.

Dried cochineal.

some synthetic red dyes.[8] Carmine was at the centre of a short-lived uproar in 2012 when vegan consumers protested Starbucks' use of it in their Strawberries and Crème Frappuccino and other products. Starbucks has since discontinued its use of carmine in favour of other natural dyes.[9]

Cochineal collecting from the host plant, a prickly pear cactus, watercolour, 1620, General Archive of the Indies, Seville, Spain.

Semi-cultivation

While few insects have been domesticated, many insect species are semi-domesticated, or semi-cultivated. Semi-cultivation refers to the human manipulation of key aspects of insect habitat in order to enhance insect reproduction for human use. Semi-cultivation includes a range of activities from simple acts (such as cutting into the bark of a tree) to increase the likelihood of an insect infestation to full-scale rearing of insects in captivity. A number of well-known historical and contemporary cases illustrate these human–insect relationships. These insect-farming methods are of increasing interest to scholars as finding sustainable ways to produce insect foods could be a source of food security and economic development for rural populations.[10]

Ahuautle

Ahuautle, or 'seeds of joy', was an important Aztec food. Ahuautle are the eggs of several aquatic true bug species, known as water boatmen (genera of the Corixidae and Notonecta families); the adults are called *axayácatl*.[11] This delicacy is hard to find nowadays and expensive, so they are sometimes referred to as 'Mexican caviar'. In the mid-sixteenth century, however, they were abundant. The naturalist Francisco Hernández noted how people living on the shores of Lake Texcoco collected, processed and consumed these and other aquatic insects:

> It looks like a poppy seed, and it is the eggs of the *axacayácatl* . . . It is gathered by throwing into the lake, where the waters are most turbulent, loosely twisted cables as

Backswimmer or water boatman (*Notonecta viridis*) in a pond at the water's surface. It is one of the many Notonectidae and Corixidae whose eggs compose *ahuautle*.

thick as a man's arm or thigh. The [eggs], shaken and swirled, adhere to these, from which the fishermen remove them and store them in large vessels. They make tortillas [from it] similar to corn ones, or the balls they call tamales . . . or they save it, split into portions and wrapped in corn husks, toasting or cooking it at a later time.[12]

A 1550 map of Lake Texcoco suggests that the Aztecs divided the lake with a reed barrier and used the shallow side for raising eggs of the water bug.[13] Into the nineteenth century observers noted that the Aztecs formed bundles of reeds which they placed a metre apart in the shallow waters of the lake. A rock secured to the bundle would make it sink to the lake floor, where the female would oviposit eggs. Weeks later, the egg-covered bundles could be pulled from the lake, dried, and the eggs quickly shaken off onto a cloth. Large quantities (literally tons) of *ahuautle* could be harvested this way. The ahuautle could then be ground and mixed with chicken eggs and fried to make cakes that were sold in marketplaces.[14]

Palm Weevil

Palm weevils are the larvae of a number of beetle species (Curculionidae family) found throughout the tropics. Many peoples, historically and today, cut into or felled palm trees specifically to facilitate weevil infestation. The Jotï, subsistence farmers and foragers in the Venezuelan Amazon, make use of a number of palm weevil species. To increase the quantity of one choice species (*Rhynchophorus palmarum*), the Jotï make deep cuts into palm bark to attract the weevils, which can be harvested a month or so later. Similar strategies are used by forest-dwelling populations from Paraguay to western

Edible larvae of the red palm weevil beetle (*Rhyncophorus ferrugineus*).

Adult red palm beetle weevil (*Rhyncophorus ferrugineus*).

Preparing a sandwich with shea caterpillars, Burkina Faso.

Papua New Guinea, where palm trees provide fruit, starch and building materials – as well as the possibility of enhancing a predictable supply of palm weevil larvae.[15]

Those who use palm trees solely for agriculture (palm oil, dates) or ornamentation dread infestations of palm weevils, which can devastate plantations and landscapes. In Southeast Asia, however, they are farmed for food and supplemental income. In southern Thailand, for instance, farmers raise red palm weevils by cutting sago or cabbage palm trunks into sections and then drilling holes into the sections. Adult palm weevil beetles are released into the logs and covered with leaves. Six weeks later palm weevils can be harvested. Because they are a nutritional powerhouse, and a much-appreciated food, several organizations are exploring the intensification of palm weevil cultivation through the construction of rearing structures or containerized production.[16]

Fresh palm weevils are described as creamy, woodsy and sweet when raw, and nutty or bacon-like when boiled and fried. The ones I purchased via mail order from Thailand came dehydrated, with a chewy texture and raisin-like taste.

Catering to Caterpillars

A number of butterfly and moth species (Lepidoptera order) are also cultivated for their edible caterpillars; these are an especially popular food in Africa, where over forty edible species have been reported for the Democratic Republic of the Congo alone. To facilitate the observation and collection of mature caterpillars, some people in the country buy or relocate leaf-feeding caterpillars to appropriate trees close to their homes. In fact, people follow a number of forest management practices that can enhance caterpillar yields, as is

the case with the mopane worm. Those interested in increasing caterpillar populations may plant specific species of host trees or manage tree/insect species through burning practices that preserve moth eggs on leaves and pupae underground, or that may protect specific breeding sites.[17] Social regulations on when and how caterpillars can be collected also serve to maintain high insect populations.

In Burkina Faso, Charlotte Payne and her colleagues have been exploring the possibility of increasing the availability of one caterpillar to help fight malnutrition in that country.[18] The shea caterpillar (*Cirina butyrospermi*) feeds, unsurprisingly, on shea trees that grow across western and sub-Saharan Africa. Women and children collect the nuts from the trees for shea butter, which has numerous culinary and cosmetic uses. They also collect the shea caterpillars when they appear in large numbers during the rainy season. Known locally as *chitoumou*, the caterpillars are very popular. They are eaten and sold in markets for additional income. Because *chitoumou* have a very short season and feed only on shea leaves, there are steep challenges involved in devising farming strategies that will increase their yield.[19]

Commercial Insect Farming

In North America, insects such as waxworms (Pyralidae family), crickets (Gryllidae family) and mealworms (*Tenebrio molitor*) have long been farmed for pet food, fishing bait and feed for other animals, but farming insects for human consumption is recent, as is the availability of insect-based foods on the market. In the 1990s, the only commercialized insect-food product that most Americans could buy was a lollipop called Hotlix. Billed as America's 'original edible insect candy

Hotlix lollipop, an example of a hard sweet or candy embedded with insects, in this case crickets and ants.

creator', Larry Peterman bought the Hotlix candy shop, known for its cinnamon candies, in Pismo Beach, California, in 1986. Although Peterman had an interest in edible insects, his first bug products were novelty items. The flagship product is a tequila-flavoured sucker embedded with a mealworm; later the company added crickets and scorpions to their lollipops.

Today there are many insect food products on the U.S. and European markets. The Belgian company Beetles Beer makes a beer flavoured with insects; and Jiminis, based in France, sells a large range of whole insects and insect-based snacks. Bug-based burgers and breads are made by Dutch and German companies. Anders Enström maintains a running list of edible insect products and companies at www.bugburger.se,

but it is not an easy industry to keep up to date with as start-ups come and go. Investors, including major agribusiness corporations like Cargill and McDonalds, have enough faith in the potential of commercial insect foods that they are putting their money into efforts to scale up production, but mass rearing of insects entails health, hygiene and safety challenges, as with any livestock production.

Farming insects for food and feed offers the possibility of generating high-quality protein at low environmental cost – and we need it given the projection of a world population of 9.8 billion by 2050. With rising income levels in some parts of the world, the global consumer demand for meat products is expected to increase. Meanwhile, our agriculture resources and ability to produce food are threatened by climate catastrophe. In comparison to conventional livestock, insects are far more efficient converters of feed to meat. As

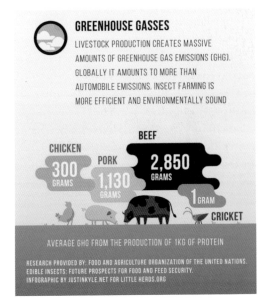

Infographic from Little Herds detailing greenhouse gas emission levels of various animals.

GREENHOUSE GASSES

LIVESTOCK PRODUCTION CREATES MASSIVE AMOUNTS OF GREENHOUSE GAS EMISSIONS (GHG). GLOBALLY IT AMOUNTS TO MORE THAN AUTOMOBILE EMISSIONS. INSECT FARMING IS MORE EFFICIENT AND ENVIRONMENTALLY SOUND

CHICKEN **300** GRAMS

PORK **1,130** GRAMS

BEEF **2,850** GRAMS

CRICKET **1 GRAM**

AVERAGE GHG FROM THE PRODUCTION OF 1KG OF PROTEIN

RESEARCH PROVIDED BY: FOOD AND AGRICULTURE ORGANIZATION OF THE UNITED NATIONS. EDIBLE INSECTS: FUTURE PROSPECTS FOR FOOD AND FEED SECURITY. INFOGRAPHIC BY JUSTINKYLE.NET FOR LITTLE HERDS.ORG cold-blooded animals, insects convert more of the energy they consume into body mass versus animals who need to maintain warm body temperature, and therefore they require fewer energy and resource inputs. Insects can be raised in crowded conditions, so they require less land. Currently, more than two-thirds of all agricultural land is used for animal production (including sheltering animals and growing feed crops for them). Livestock production alone is responsible for 15 per cent of all human-generated greenhouse gasses when the complete agricultural process – from grain-feed production, to raising animals, to processing and shipping their products – is taken into account.[20] Mass production of insects might be a way to produce more high-quality protein with a much smaller environmental footprint than conventional meat.

Wageningen University in the Netherlands is a hub for research and experimentation regarding edible insects in Europe where researchers developed early commercial farming methods and efforts towards engaging the Dutch public in eating insects through events like the City of Insects festival and an Insect Experience Festival.[21]

Scaling Up: Small Farms and Factory Farms

In the realm of insect farming for human consumption, crickets have been the object of most of the attention. Thailand is a leader in the field and has been called 'the home of cricket farming'. Starting only a few decades ago via a project at the Kwon Kaen University, there are now an estimated 20,000 families engaged in cricket farming. Crickets provide income and opportunities for tens of thousands of people who process, transport and market the crickets.

Cricket farm, Thailand.

Most Thai cricket farms are still small-scale, selling to regional wholesalers and to vendors who offer fried crickets as a street food alongside other insect snacks popular in Thai cities. Urban demand is increasing, however, as large supermarkets enter the market for crickets, creating the potential for larger-scale industrial operations. One company, EIF (Edible Insect Foods), located in Chiang Mai, manufactures cricket products for export to Europe.[22] Perhaps to facilitate industrial development as well as opportunities for exportation, Thailand recently formulated a set of GAP (Good Agricultural Practices) guidelines to improve on-farm hygienic standards.[23]

North American producers have also bet on the cricket as the first widely marketed insect for human consumption. Crickets provide lean protein and a bland taste that can easily be combined with other ingredients. Cricket powder (from roasted and ground crickets) is currently used in a number of processed food items, such as protein bars, biscuits and crisps (chips), and is sold on its own. The first cricket farm in the u.s. licensed to sell food-grade insects was Big Cricket Farms in Youngstown, Ohio, founded by a young entrepreneur, Kevin Bachhuber. Bachhuber was initially interested in economic revitalization and landed on cricket farming as a sustainable route forward. Local water problems eventually caused him to close. But many other farms have since popped up around the country and no wonder – ground cricket powder costs some u.s.$35 per 450 grams (1 lb). It is far more expensive than other protein powders on the market.

Entomo Farms in Canada is another leading producer. Entomo Farms is a family operation that began as a reptile-feed supplier, but transitioned in 2013 to producing crickets

Bugsolutely cricket powder pasta.

for human consumption. Their 5,570-square-metre (60,000 sq. ft) production space is North America's largest human-grade cricket farm,[24] and their website claims that crickets are the 'planet's most sustainable super-food'. Entomo sells cricket powder, whole roasted crickets and flavoured crickets. They also sell plain and flavoured mealworms. Entomo markets 'Chili Lime Crickets' as a topping for salads or rice bowls or as a crunchy snack. At u.s.$24 for a 115-gram (4 oz) package,[25] the crickets are a very expensive alternative to conventional North American protein sources. The cost reflects both the real cost of production and the low supply and high demand for cricket products.

Edible insects may provide a healthy, greener alternative to conventional meat, but the industry is not big enough yet to be a real challenge to conventional protein sources. Aspire Food Group, however, aims to increase their cricket production dramatically. Aspire was founded in 2012 by five McGill University students who won the million-dollar Hult Prize, a prestigious student competition to solve the world's greatest challenges. In 2017 Aspire set up a fully automated cricket-breeding facility in Austin, Texas. With increasing production and decreasing costs, the price may come down for consumers as well as for global food corporations who will want to manufacture insect foods.[26] In 2018 Aspire acquired the brand exo, a New York-based start-up and an early producer of high-protein cricket powder snack bars.

Although the claims for environmental sustainability are a key part of marketing new cricket (and other insect) foods, there is scant data on how 'green' such products are in reality. Insects may not need energy to regulate their body temperature, but in higher latitudes they require energy-intensive temperature-controlled environments. Crickets prefer temperatures between 26 and 32 degrees Celsius (78.8–89.6°F).

For insects to survive and be nutritious for humans, they also require nutrient-dense feed. Researchers found that crickets in industrial-scale production could only be successfully raised on high-quality feed (that is, feed based on cultivated grains, similar to that conventionally fed to poultry).[27] With this input requirement, crickets showed little improvement in protein conversion efficiency over poultry. From an environmental standpoint it is better to eat our cultivated grains and legumes directly rather than turn them into feed.

Other massive-scale insect farms are not for human food per se. Cockroaches raised primarily for pharmaceutical purposes are a booming business in China and are raised in large indoor breeding facilities. One such farm in southwestern Sichuan Province is the largest in the world, rearing 6 billion cockroaches per year in a high-tech breeding facility that uses artificial intelligence to control temperature, humidity, feed supply and consumption, tracking eighty categories of 'big data'. The cockroaches (*Periplaneta americana*) are used by the pharmaceutical industry for remedies in traditional Chinese medicine, such as a popular remedy to treat stomach pain and other ailments. According to a Chinese government report, the farm generated U.S.$684 million selling the popular remedy.[28] One cannot help but wonder about the consequences of a massive cockroach leak. In 2013, in fact, a million cockroaches escaped from a farm in southeastern China after someone sabotaged the breeding facility.

Black Soldier Fly

The true environmental benefits of insect foods could be realized if the insects we raised for foods lived on substances that humans cannot eat, like excrement, beer mash or toxic algae. What if they cleaned up our waste while also producing a nutrient-dense food and feed source? Enter the black soldier fly (*Hermetia illucens*), or 'BSF'. Adult BSF are a globally widespread species of black-coloured fly, less than 2.5 centimetres (1 in.) in length. They are neither a pest nor harmful to humans. The adults mate and lay eggs and do not eat anything; all their energy has been saved up from their larval stage.

The larvae of this fly will eat almost anything – and they do so voraciously. They start off as eggs no bigger than a fleck of ground black pepper, and in the fourteen days from the time they hatch until they pupate each larva increases its body weight 10,000-fold, which is 'akin to an eight pound baby swelling to a 40-ton humpback whale' as one report put it.[29] Entomologists have known about BSF's power to convert wastes, even manure, into protein for decades but only recently

An adult black soldier fly (*Hermetia illucens*).

Black soldier fly larvae (*Hermetia illucens*).

discovered the right environmental controls needed to be able to breed them in captivity on a large scale. That discovery has allowed for the development of a number of breeding facilities and commercial applications, and the future is promising. Because millions of the 'worms' can be raised in stacked bins, they are far more productive per acre than other protein sources. In one year, for instance, a single acre of black soldier fly larvae can produce more protein than 3,000 acres of cattle or 130 acres of soybeans.

The Evo company in Texas raises BSF grubs on tons of spent distillery grain; and in China the company JM Green uses BSF to process 50 tons of food waste per day. When the larvae reach maturity, they are harvested and dried and processed into oil and protein meal that can be used in a variety of industrial products and animal feed. Their waste is a rich compost that can be used in landscaping.

While the larvae (and pupae) are edible for people, and those raising them are happy to chomp on a few baked and salted maggots, BSF larvae are not currently commercially raised for human consumption, in part due to concerns about transmission of pathogens present in the waste stream. Food safety regulations in many countries, however, have begun to allow BSF products into feed for animals meant for human consumption. In the U.S., BSF protein meal is now allowed for poultry and fish feed. BSF meal can lessen our reliance on traditional sources of protein meal, such as fishmeal from over-exploited fisheries. The giants of the global food system, including Cargill, are betting on a productive and profitable future for BSF.

The little black soldier fly might be our hero; they sequester the carbon in rotting food waste, turn it to fat and protein for animals and leave behind only compost. Perhaps one day we will eat BSF burgers. Until then, researchers evaluating the ecological efficiency of insects note that the greatest savings in agricultural resources and reduction of greenhouse gas emissions can be had by simply reducing consumption of all animal products and shifting to a plant-based diet. So, if you want to follow a diet that is good for the planet, eat mostly plants and choose crickets in place of your hamburger. You might also look for your local distillery or brewery, ask if there is a BSF farm around and drink up.

6

The Insectivore's Dilemma

Designer Katharina Unger imagines a world where even apartment dwellers can raise insects for their own household consumption. Her Farm 432 is a tabletop, black-soldier-fly-larvae breeding machine that provides climate-controlled chambers for adult flies to breed and for the subsequent larvae to grow, be harvested for food and used to start the process again. This prototype BSF breeder would allow people to harvest some 500 grams (17½ oz) of larvae, enough for two meals per week. The larvae she has raised and cooked so far, she says, 'smell a bit like cooked potatoes. The consistency is a bit harder on the outside and like soft meat on the inside. The taste is nutty and a bit meaty.'[1] Although her Farm 432 for BSF is still in development, Unger's tabletop farm for mealworms, the Hive, is on the market via her Hong Kong-based company Livin Farms.

The Hive is a climate-controlled unit with eight drawers, fans and a filter. The top drawer is for pupae. Once they grow into adult beetles, they mate and lay eggs which fall through small perforations in the bottom of the drawer and into the next. There the eggs hatch into larvae, that is, the mealworms, and are fed kitchen scraps such as carrot ends and potato peels. At the push of a button, the unit vibrates to separate mealworms from waste. Once the mealworms make it all the way to the bottom drawer, which chills them, they are ready to harvest. Livin Farms estimates that an up-and-running farm will produce an average of 350 grams (1–2 U.S. cups) of mealworms per week, enough for three or four meals.

Ento-preneurs and innovators are working hard to convince consumers in the West that there are good reasons for eating insects. It turns out that even the most sympathetic would-be consumers, who want to incorporate insects into their diets for their nutritional qualities and environmental efficiencies, may find themselves wrestling with a deeply rooted 'ick' factor. This has been called the 'insectivore's dilemma':[2] one may know all the nutritional and environmental arguments for eating insects and still not want to take a bite. Many entopreneurs are banking on the trendiness of insect foods to get consumers to take that first bite, but perhaps they are on the wrong track.

Deliciousness

Philosopher Ophelia Deroy, chef Ben Reade and the experimental psychologist Charles Spence all argue that the effectiveness of health and environmental arguments for eating insects is limited at best.[3] What experts tell us we *should* eat is often not what we *do* eat. The problem is rarely one of education. We know that broccoli is better for us than crisps but still eat the crisps; and most people have less resistance to broccoli than to insects. Deroy and her collaborators argue that the way to potential insectivores' hearts is not through their minds but through their senses.

René Redzepi, chef and owner of the world-famous restaurant Noma, in Copenhagen, agrees. 'Unless the world is coming to an end and there is nothing else to eat, if it is not delicious, you don't get people to eat it. If it is delicious, it's a whole different story . . . It is all about deliciousness, deliciousness, and deliciousness.' Redzepi believes that Westerners will only adopt insects if they are actually delicious and that much work needs to happen in the kitchen before consumers will really want to regularly eat insects. He remarks that

> meat is full of umami; it is juicy. A cricket, just fried, is crunchy and there is not a lot of flavor. Some are perfectly good as breadcrumbs: they can be dried and ground to a powder, and then you can roll carrots in it and fry them in butter. The result is browned and tasty. But right now, to eat insects as a meal, I believe we need a lot more experimenting, a lot more iconic dishes that taste really good for people to be persuaded.[4]

Redzepi has tried many insects and, crickets aside, it is the taste of insects that has persuaded Redzepi and other chefs to eat them.

Alex Atala, a Brazilian chef and founder of the renowned restaurant D.O.M in São Paulo, agrees. Atala experienced the Amazonian forest as a boy on his family's farm. He later backpacked through Europe and worked in kitchens, eventually becoming a chef fully trained in classical French techniques. Returning to Brazil, he began substituting Brazilian ingredients for European ones, partly out of the necessity to make do with the ingredients available to him, but also due to his growing sense that native Brazilian foods have great gastronomic potential. They are delicious and sophisticated in their own right although wholly underappreciated and often ignored in haute cuisine. Atala travelled to explore the tastes of his own vast country. One visit to the Amazon brought him in touch with Dona Brazi, an indigenous woman and cook from the town of São Gabriel das Cachoeiras. Trying some of her delicious food he asked,

'Which herbs did you put into this dish?'
She replied, 'Ants.'
Since she did not speak Portuguese well, Atala assumed she had not understood his question, he repeated, 'I would like to know which HERBS you used in this recipe.'
She had understood him perfectly well: 'Son, there's only ants.'[5]

Atala was enchanted by the ants' strong taste of lemongrass, ginger and cardamom.

These ants, leafcutter ants (*Atta* spp.), are one of a number of edible ant species native to South America. They turned out to be a culinary key, opening Atala's mind to other unknown and underutilized ingredients. Atala carried these ants abroad

Leaf cutter ant (*Atta* sp).

Brazilian chef Alex Atala and his golden ant meringue.

to use in presentations about the need to valorize local knowledge and local ingredients. Halfway across the world, at a MAD symposium in Denmark, Atala shared his ants with Redzepi, who was amazed at the taste. Already at the forefront of promoting cuisine with local natural and seasonal produce, Redzepi began exploring the taste realm of insects as food.

The Insect Project became a major research effort at Redzepi's Nordic Food Lab, the renowned centre for gastronomic experimentation. The Lab's book, *On Eating Insects*, is a beautiful and thought-provoking collection of essays by the Insect Project team of chefs, social scientists and food scientists. The essays follow the team's journey around the world to document insects' gastronomic potential. Theirs is perhaps the first book on insect foods to take taste seriously and to treat insects as ingredients worthy of the world's most sophisticated haute cuisine. If you fancy yourself a foodie, the luxurious photos and tasting notes will make you want to eat bugs. They write that the Thai lychee stink bug (*Tessaratoma papillosa*) tastes like 'Kaffir lime, coriander, apple skin with sweet notes of banana and tropical fruits', while the Japanese giant hornet (*Vespa mandarinia*) tastes 'strong, meaty, chewy, animal, pungent'.[6] They also provide recipes, but most are not for the home cook (unless you are used to making your own garum, or fermented fish sauce, and own a Thermomix and an immersion circulator).

Redzepi, the Nordic Lab members, and Atala are among the chefs redefining the West's relationship with insect foods by making them gourmet ingredients. To discover what is delicious, not just edible, they have turned to the billions of people in the world today who appreciate their taste, and know how to find, raise, prepare and combine them with other ingredients in the context of traditional cuisines. Few of the commercialized insect-based foods available on the market today capitalize on insects' flavour potential.

Not a Panacea

Insect foods have been touted as 'the last great hope to save the planet' – a solution to hunger and malnutrition as well as a low-threshold route to economic development for vulnerable populations.[7] Insects can certainly provide both nutritious and sustainable food and feed for a growing planet, but they are not a panacea. This presents the would-be insectivore with another dilemma: how to ensure that the potential benefits of eating insects actually come to pass.

As the farming of some insects in Europe and North America scales up, more efficient breeding and ecologically friendly rearing methods may be found; but there is no reason to think that this technological know-how will necessarily lead to sustainability or more food resources for all. As some critics have asked:

> What if the same will happen to insects as with other [so-called] super-, eco- and solution foods like soy? Once commodified and circulating within world markets, partly serving as feed for livestock rather than being eaten directly, they were often displaced from their former cultural embedding and after all did not benefit the poor and underprivileged. Nor did they necessarily lead to sustainable production, despite their potential to do so.[8]

Cricket powder and other insect products are already much like other ingredients in a global market: novel ingredients used only to create new snacks for an already overfed consumer.

As revolutionary as eating insects might seem to Europeans and Americans, insect foods in and of themselves do not necessarily address the root problem of sustainable

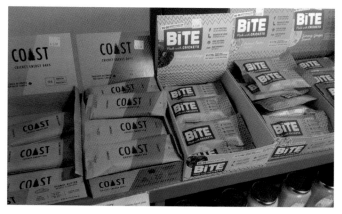

Insect-based snack foods.

production and hunger alleviation: inequality. In many parts of the world, wild insects have been collected, prepared and sold by people who hold little economic or political power. While an expanding market might mean opportunities for these communities, it might also mean that they sell this nutritious food source rather than eating it, thereby exacerbating nutritional deficiencies.

In Southeast Asia, the sociologist Andrew Müller documented many of the problems with growing insect production and trade.[9] Müller observed that a loss of insect habitats within Thailand, coupled with increasing demand for insects from urbanites, resulted in the importation of insects from the neighbouring countries of Myanmar, Laos and Cambodia, where insects are also important foodstuffs. The problem is that these bordering nations have higher rates of malnourishment than Thailand. Thus, he says, insects that were key sources of protein in the meagre diets of rural peasants ended up being eaten (mostly as snacks) by already well-fed city dwellers in Thailand and beyond. Müller also documents the monotonous labour of seasonal workers in Cambodia who process insects and earn below minimum wages for insect products that bring handsome profits to national and international entrepreneurs and middlemen. Commoditizing insects as food does not automatically mean better livelihoods for those who collect them.

Conservation efforts are vital to preserve insects, ecosystems and local foods. Transparent trade and labelling are important too, so that consumers can know where, how and by whom wild foodstuffs are collected. Without these measures, many vulnerable people in the world, who continue to quietly and regularly include insects in their daily fare, may find that global capital and new markets have taken this food right out of their mouths.

One Insect Eater's Journey

At 'Eating Insects Detroit' in 2016, North America's first conference of scholars, scientists, entrepreneurs and others focused on the future of edible insects, I sampled an array of the insect-based snack foods, pasta, powders and meat products now more widely available. All were palatable, but the truely *toothsome* were provided by Paul Landkamer, a master naturalist who resides in Missouri. Landkamer frequently speaks at public events about edible insects and runs two Facebook groups: Missouri Entomophagy and Wild Edibles of Missouri. Among many commercial products, Paul's small display and tray of wild edibles caught my eye. He stood with chopsticks in hand, talking to passers-by, ready to serve one of the June bugs, grasshoppers, Japanese beetles or caterpillars he had caught and prepared with his various marinades.

I tried a June bug and Japanese beetle. They were tasty, crunchy bites. I could imagine them sprinkled on a salad. Paul sent me a copy of his cookbook, 26 typed pages of recipes and notes. Since eating them, I have looked differently on those pesky June bugs that flit about my porch light on Midwestern summer nights. I have not yet harvested them because they are not as numerous as they were when I was a child. I have, however, harvested Japanese beetles (*Popillia japonica*, an invasive species that has infested landscapes across the United States) and prepared them following Paul's recipes.

I also decided to raise and eat my own mealworms, but did so without fancy equipment such as the Livin Hive. Many poultry farmers and pet owners raise mealworms to feed their chickens, pet reptiles, birds and hedgehogs, and they have provided instructions for home-built systems. My farm is made from three plastic bins with lids. The critters need

The wild-caught edible insects of Paul Landkamer, a Missouri
entomophagist.

plenty of airflow, so using a utility knife and duct tape, I cut
the centre out of the lids and secured a nylon window screen
over the holes. The screen keeps other bugs out of my mealworm bins. Three bins are required to keep the developmental
stages of the mealworms separate, otherwise adults and
larvae will eat developing pupae. I ordered the darkling

beetles (*Tenebrio molitor*) online and the company sent me a starter kit with larvae (the mealworms), pupae and adult beetles. Filling each bin with a few cups of oats, some wheatbran and a piece of apple, I began the micro-ranch in my mud room. They require periodic maintenance, but I do not mind sorting out the pupae and putting them into their own bin. Darkling beetles do not bite or sting and rarely fly. I grew

Japanese beetles (*Popillia japonica*) being boiled in preparation for dehydration.

Home-raised mealworms (*Tenebrio molitar*) on tomato soup.

affectionate towards my 'darklings.' After several weeks I was ready to harvest fresh, organic, home-raised mealworms.

After sorting out the mature larvae, I killed them by freezing. When I was ready to eat them, I took them out of the freezer, washed them and boiled them briefly in salted water. I then sautéed them in a hot frying pan with a bit of grapeseed oil. Their tiny legs and 'squirming' movement in

My mealworm farm.

the hot oil was off-putting, I will admit, but the aroma was enticing. Draining them on towels, I added salt and pepper and did not hesitate to taste them . . . they were delicious. Crispy, chewy, nutty.

Sadly, few friends take me up on my offer to prepare mealworm treats for them, and colleagues at university eye my potluck or shared lunch contributions warily. Despite my successful experiments and experiences with edible insects, I myself do not eat them regularly. I am however more curious than ever about insects as food and hope that future travels take me to the fields and kitchens where insects are caught and prepared. I will not hesitate to partake.

Why Eat Insects?

For me, the best reason to eat insects, and the one most rarely discussed, is that it changes one's relation to them intellectually and emotionally. At least that is my experience. Of course, eating them is not *required* for this change of heart towards the critters, but eating insects encourages you to think about what you eat, where it comes from and why you eat.

Curiosity about rather than rejection of insect foods also cultivates respect for the billions of people today (and in the past) who eat them and understand their taste, life cycles, means of harvest and ways of preparation. The world's diverse food cultures reflect detailed ecological knowledge that is fast disappearing with the loss of biodiversity and habitat.

Chef Alex Atala's use of insects and native foods was always about more than their flavour: 'behind that flavour there is a culture and to strengthen that culture is perhaps the main mission of this work.'[10] Atala started the ATA Institute, whose manifesto reads:

> the relation between man and food must be revised. We need to bring knowledge closer to eating, eating to cooking, cooking to producing, producing to nature; working along the whole value chain to strengthen landscapes in their biodiversity, agrodiversity and socio-diversity, to ensure good food for all and to preserve the environment.[11]

Insects are the root of life, essential for all ecosystems, but they are vanishing at a shockingly rapid rate. Nearly 40 per cent of insect species are in decline and one-third of them are in danger of extinction due to pesticide use, urbanization and climate change.[12] Those in the West do not need to eat insects to save the planet, but we do need to preserve habitats to forestall the catastrophic loss of services that their extinctions will engender. We need to rethink our relationship with insects because our lives depend on it. We cannot survive without them.

Recipes

The first step for the would-be insect chef is to acquire insects. For those who want to collect wild insects, a local entomology society will be a great resource for identifying and locating edible species in natural areas free of pesticides and herbicides. There are also plenty of mail order marketplaces offering an increasingly varied selection of insects reared specifically for human consumption, although these are usually dehydrated or otherwise processed for long-term preservation in a way that completely changes the insects' taste and possible uses. As with any unfamilar food, people should seek out a knowledgeable guide. Never put insect foods before diners who are unaware or try to 'sneak' them into a recipe. Everyone consumes insects at their own risk and benefit. Most sources warn that people who are allergic to shellfish should also avoid ingesting insects.

Historical Preparations

Giant Water-bug Essence (*Cà Cuống*)
A traditional preparation as described by Pierre Huard
and Maurice M. Durand, *Connaissance du Viêt-Nam* (1990), trans.
Vu Thiên Kim, see https://ehrafworldcultures.yale.edu

In North Vietnam, a pungent flavouring is extracted from fluid-filled vesicles, the size of rice grains, located in the abdomen of males of the species. The liquid is a pheromone used by the males to attract females. Traditionally this water bug 'essence' was gathered by women and children who extract, with the use of a fine pin, the two liquid-filled sacs. These are preserved in saltwater. Huard and Durand found that a few drops of this liquid 'suffice to raise the taste and flavour of any aliment' but that *cà cuống* essence was particularly utilized in pickling brine, shrimp preserves, and the dipping sauces for *bánh cưng* (sticky rice cakes) for *bánh cuốn* (steamed rice rolls). Artificially flavoured substitutes are common in Vietnam today.

Palm Weevil
From Peter Lund, *The Curiosities of Food; or, The Dainties
and Delicacies of Different Nations Obtained from the
Animal Kingdom* (London, 1859)

Richard Brookes, in *On the Properties and Uses of Insects* (1772), reports of palm weevils (*Rhynchophorus ferrugineus*):

> They are eaten by the French, in the West Indies, after they have been roasted before the fire, when a small wooden spit has been thrust through them. When they begin to be hot, they powder them with a crust of rasped bread, mixed with salt, and a little pepper and nutmeg. This powder keeps in the fat or at least, sucks it up: and when they are done enough, they are served up with orange juice. They are highly esteemed by the French as excellent eating.

Locust Broth (1877)

From Charles Riley, *First Annual Report of the United States Entomological Commission for the Year 1877: Relating to the Rocky Mountain Locust and the Best Methods of Preventing Its Injuries and of Guarding against Its Invasions, in Pursuance of an Appropriation Made by Congress for This Purpose* (Washington, DC, 1877)

Charles V. Riley, first director of the U.S. Entomological Commission, argued that locusts needed little preparation or seasoning, that frying or roasting them in their own fat with a bit of salt made them palatable. Yet he supposed that eating them this way would not be as wholesome as in a broth or soup. He suggested the following:

> A broth, made by boiling the unfledged *Calopteni* [now *Melanoplus*] for two hours in the proper quantity of water, and seasoned with nothing in the world but pepper and salt, is quite palatable, and can scarcely be distinguished from beef broth, though it has a slight flavor peculiar to it, and not easily described. The addition of a little butter improves it, and the flavor can, of course, be modified with mint, sage, or other spices *ad libitum.*

Khoi Locust Milk (early 1900s)

From Leonhard Sigmund Schultze, *Un Namaland und Kalahari* (1907), trans. Elizabeth C. Knight and Theodore Ziolkowski for the Human Relations Area Files, see https://ehrafworldcultures.yale.edu

Leonhard Sigmund Schultze, a zoologist at the University of Jena, conducted fieldwork from 1903 to 1907 in the area of the Khoi people in the Kalahari. He describes a special food prepared by women during occasions of desert locust outbreaks:

> When [the female locusts, full of eggs] have retired to their nocturnal quarters . . . and hang massed together on the branches, the Hottentot [now Khoi] sets fire to the

bush. It flares up all over. The next morning the ashes are swept up with branches, gathered up in skins and spread out on large flat rocks. The insects with eggs are sorted out. The others are only collected if there are not enough of the ones with eggs. The collected insects are put in sacks and brought to the huts on oxen. There the mass is spread out, women sit in a circle around it and pulverize it with stones. When it is prepared, the soft light brown mass is loaded into skin sacks and stored. When stirred up with milk it is supposed to be better tasting than when raw.

Contemporary Recipes

(Real) Ants on a (Fake) Log Two Ways

'Ants on a Log' refers to a North American children's snack of celery sticks (the logs) slathered with peanut butter and topped with raisins (the ants), but it has also been an irresistible inspiration for bug chefs who use real ants on a variety of 'logs'.

The most complex version I have found was created by chef Josh Pollen of the Nordic Food Lab (now part of the Future Consumer lab at the University of Copenhagen); it was originally called the 'Chimp Stick', inspired, of course, by chimpanzees' resourceful use of sticks to gather termites. A version of the Nordic Lab's 'Chimp Stick' recipe on BugsFeed.com calls for: liquorice roots, whittled such that one end is stripped of bark; honey infused overnight with juniper wood; and local ants (*Formica rufa* and *Lasius fuliginosus* specifically, although these might not be local in your area), frozen within an hour of harvesting. The one-end-stripped liquorice root is coated lightly with the honey. Other ingredients (toasted buckwheat groats, golden linseeds, freeze-dried raspberry pieces, small leaves of purple shiso and coriander cress, and small cherry blossoms) are stuck in a scattered fashion along it. The Nordic Lab has also provided the following slightly simpler version.

Ants on a Log (Nordic Food Lab Version)

From Nordic Food Lab, www.nordicfoodlab.org,
and licensed under a Creative Commons
Attribution-ShareAlike 4.0 International Licence

400 g celeriac
40 g butter
2 g birch bud salt
50 g celeriac peel, reserved
1 g coffee grounds
50 g rye bread, sweet dark, dried
250 g sunflower seeds
250 g water, filtered
50 g sunflower oil, cold-pressed
2 g sea salt
16 lovage leaves
40 sweet cicely (garden myrrh) leaves
160 carpenter ants (*Lasius fuliginosus*)

For the log:

Peel the celeriac, reserving the outer peel. Slice the celeriac into 3-cm-thick slices, cut the slices into long batons 3 cm square and shape the batons into cylinders. Slight imperfection is desirable. Heat the butter until the milk solids caramelize to a golden brown and remove from the heat and cool. Add the brown butter to a sous vide bag with the celeriac cylinders and season with birch bud salt, seal and cook at 85 °C for 30–40 minutes until soft and melting but still retaining texture.

For the bark crumb:

In a preheated oven, char the celeriac peel at 300 °C for 10 minutes, allow to cool and pass through a fine sieve to create an ash.

Blend the rye bread crumb into a fine powder, and mix with a little of the celeriac ash and ground coffee to create a bark for the celeriac log.

For the sunflower seed butter:
Roast the sunflower seeds at 160°C for 10 minutes, cover with the water and soak overnight in the fridge. The next day, drain the seeds, reserving 100 g of the soaking liquid. In a Pacojet container, blast-freeze the seeds together with the reserved soaking liquid and sunflower oil. When fully frozen, blend, re-freeze and re-blend until you have a smooth cream. Taste and adjust the seasoning if necessary. [One could also purchase sunflower butter.]

Garnish:
Pick the youngest, smallest lovage and sweet cicely leaves.

To serve:
Roll the celeriac log in the bark crumb until fully coated. Shake off excess. Trim ends flat to reveal the clean white wood. Place on plate, and place at least 40 ants on the log, or more if you can manage. There should be none on the plate. Spoon a small mound of roasted sunflower seed cream near to the log, and arrange the sweet cicely and lovage leaves so that it resembles a small fern.

Ants on a Log (All Things Jerky® Version)
From All Things Jerky®, allthingsjerky.com, used with permission

This fast-food version of ants on a log was a hit at the 2018 Wisconsin State Fair.

large pretzel sticks
a jar of marshmallow fluff
dehydrated black ants and/or queen weaver ants

Dip large pretzel logs into jar of marshmallow fluff to thoroughly coat two-thirds of the stick. Spread black ants or queen weaver ants (or a combination of the two) in a thin layer on a plate. Lightly roll marshmallowed pretzel in ants.

Deep-fried Tarantulas (1998)
From David George Gordon, *Eat-a-bug Cookbook*
(Berkeley, CA, 1998), used with permission

This deep-fried tarantula recipe comes from 'the Bug Chef', David George Gordon, and won him the championship at the 2011 Big Bug Cook-off at the Natural History Museum of Los Angeles County. Rather than the wok-fried versions seen in Cambodia, Gordon's is a battered and deep-fried tarantula tempura. It is a simple enough recipe but requires some preparation. According to Gordon's recipe, the tarantulas must be gutted and de-haired before they are battered and deep fried. He suggests cutting the spider in two lengthwise and sprinkling with paprika to serve.

2 cups (500 ml) of canola or vegetable oil
2 frozen adult Texas brown, Chilean rose or similar-sized tarantulas, thawed
1 cup (200 g) tempura batter
1 tsp smoked paprika

Heat oil to 350 °F (175 °C).

With a sharp knife, sever and discard the abdomens from the two tarantulas. Singe off any of the spiders' body hair with a crème brûlée torch or butane cigarette lighter.

Dip each spider into the tempura batter to thoroughly coat. Use a slotted spoon or your hands to make sure each spider's legs remain splayed – they will want to clump together – before dropping it into the hot oil.

Deep fry the spiders, one at a time, until the batter is lightly browned, about 1 minute. Remove the spider from the oil and place on paper towels to drain.

Use a sharp knife to cut each spider in two lengthwise. Sprinkle with the paprika and serve. Encourage guests to try the legs first and, if still hungry, to nibble on the meat-filled mesothorax, avoiding the spiders' paired fangs, which are tucked away in the head region.

Escamoles à la Mexicana (Ant Brood Tacos) (1998)

From Julieta Ramos-Elorduy, *Creepy Crawly Cuisine: The Gourmet Guide to Edible Insects* (Rochester, VT, 1998), used with permission

2 tbsp butter or peanut oil
½ lb (450 g) of ant larvae and pupae
3 serrano chillies, raw, finely chopped
1 medium onion, finely chopped
1 tomato, seeded and finely chopped
black pepper, to taste
cumin, to taste
oregano, to taste
1 handful of cilantro (coriander), chopped
corn tortillas

Heat butter or oil in a frying pan and fry the larvae and pupae. Add chopped onion, chillies, and tomato. Season with salt, pepper, cumin and oregano, to taste. Warm tortillas gently on a griddle. To serve, fill tortillas with escamole mix and garnish with cilantro.

Cricket Ricotta Pancakes

From Entomo Farms, https://entomofarms.com, used with permission

Entomo Farms is one of North America's premier cricket farms. The farm, located in Ontario, Canada, raises crickets and processes them into whole roasted-cricket snacks and cricket protein powder. Like other protein powders, Entomo's cricket powder can be mixed into smoothies or mixed with flour in baked goods.

1 ½ cups (200 g) all-purpose (plain) flour
¼ cup (25 g) cricket powder

3 tbsp brown sugar
1 tsp baking powder
1 tsp baking soda (bicarbonate of soda)
¼ tsp salt
2 eggs
1 cup (250 g) ricotta
1 cup (250 ml) almond milk or regular milk
1 tsp vanilla
1 tbsp safflower or rapeseed (canola) oil
½ cup (120 ml) water

In a large bowl, whisk together flour, cricket powder, brown sugar, baking powder, baking soda and salt. In a second bowl, whisk eggs. Then whisk in ricotta, milk, vanilla and oil. Make a well in flour mixture. Pour in egg mixture and stir just until combined. Add water to thin and to correct consistency. Heat a large non-stick frying pan to medium temperature. Lightly brush with remaining butter or oil if needed. When hot, scoop about ¼ cup (30 g) batter into pan. Cook until bubbles form on the top, 2 to 3 min. Flip and cook until golden brown, about 2 more minutes. Reduce heat if pancakes are browning too quickly. Remove and cover to keep warm. Serve with maple syrup or your favourite pancake topping!

Fried Mealworms

Darkling beetles are surprisingly easy to raise at home but require a small amount of regular attention to maintain their nesting cartons and to separate the pupal stage from the larval and adult stages. Numerous directions are available online for establishing a colony. Mealworms (the larval stage) can be harvested once they reach full size (2–2.5 cm/¾–1 in.). Harvest by separating mealworms from frass (excrement) and any bedding or food scraps. Freeze to kill.

When ready to use, portion out the amount of frozen mealworms to be cooked. Sort mealworms to remove oddly shaped or discoloured insects. Rinse thoroughly under running water. Boil with salt for 5 minutes.

Strain from the water. Fry in a small amount of grapeseed or other oil. Strain onto paper towel and add salt.

Serve as a topping for salad or soup.

Mealworm Chocolate Chip Cookies

Originally published in the November 1981 issue of
Creature Features, the Insect Zoo's newsletter (see the Archives'
Accession #11-203, National Museum of Natural History, Office
of Education), newsletter, used with permission

Mealworms have a slightly nutty flavour and can be used in a variety of baked goods, either whole, after roasting, or ground into a powder, as in this recipe from the Smithsonian Institution's Archives.

The recipe calls for live, bran-raised larvae that have been washed, killed by freezing or boiling, then roasted on a baking tray at 105 °C (225 °F) for 2–3 hours. After they cool, grind in a blender or food processor until they are reduced to 'a very fatty, protein-rich flour', which can be stored in the freezer until ready for use.

¾ cup (170 g) butter
1 cup (200 g) sugar
½ cup (100 g) brown sugar
12 oz (340 g) chocolate chips
2 eggs
1 tsp vanilla
⅔ cup (80 g) ground mealworms
1⅓ cup (180 g) flour
½ tsp salt
1 tsp baking soda (bicarbonate of soda)

Cream butter with sugar, eggs, and vanilla. Add combined dry ingredients, then chocolate chips. Drop by teaspoon onto a greased cookie sheet [baking tray] and bake at 375 °F (190 °C) for 8–10 minutes. Makes approximately 8 dozen cookies. Recipe may be halved.

Austrian Vanilla Crescent Cookies
with Buffalo Worm flour

From Anita Drulea, Food Insects, www.foodinsects.de,
used with permission

250 g all-purpose (plain) flour
25 g buffalo worm (*Alphitobius diaperinus*) powder
250 g butter
100 g almonds, ground
80 g sugar

For covering cookies:
1 package of icing sugar (90 g)
2 packages (8 g each) vanilla sugar

For the dough, simply knead all the ingredients together well with hands or dough mixer. Wrap dough in cling film and put it in the fridge for 30 minutes.

In the meantime, prepare the sugar. Sift the powdered sugar and mix with vanilla sugar in a shallow bowl.

Remove dough from refrigerator and roll about 4-cm-thick rolls. Cut rolls in slices 1–2 cm thick and form crescents out of them. Lay crescents on a sheet of baking paper on a baking pan. Do not crowd. Bake for 20 minutes at 175 °C in convection oven. Crisps should be nicely browned.

Remove from oven and let cool for a few minutes.

Pass the cookies while warm through the sugar mixture. It is important to have the cookies at the right temperature: if the vanilla croissants are still too warm, they break, if they are too cold, the sugar no longer sticks.

Cookies will keep in a tin for about 6 weeks.

Critter Bitter Old Fashioned (Cocktail)

Designers Lucy Knops and Julia Plevin co-founded Critter Bitters with the goal of taking the 'ick' factor out of eating insects. Their toasted cricket tincture produces a subtle essence that will not offend even the most finicky eater (or drinker, in this case). Serve the Critter Bitter Old Fashioned to apprehensive guests for whom you are preparing the other recipes in this book. Recipe used with permission.

2 oz (60 ml) bourbon or rye
¼ oz (5 ml) of agave mix (equal parts water and light agave syrup)
3 droppers full Critter Bitters

Combine ingredients in a shaker full of ice. Stir well and strain over ice in rocks glass. Garnish with orange peel and a dried cricket.

Bee Brood Granola
From Nordic Food Lab, www.nordicfoodlab.org, and licensed under a Creative Commons Attribution-ShareAlike 4.0 International Licence

Honeybee (*Apis mellifera*) brood is a delicacy in many countries, including Australia, Mexico and Thailand. The recipe below comes from the Nordic Food Lab. The first challenge of this recipe is finding bee brood, although many beekeepers routinely remove drone combs from their hives. Another challenge is harvesting the brood itself, which is very fragile and difficult to remove from the hive. Nordic Food Lab chefs suggests using liquid nitrogen to freeze the comb and then rolling the frozen bees between the hands to remove all wax and honey while leaving the bee larvae intact. Another method is to place the honeycomb with larvae into warm water to melt it and then strain the larvae out. After the first straining, boiling water can be poured over the larvae in the strainer to further rinse and separate the brood. Once you have obtained the brood, the possibilities are endless. For the granola, the Nordic Lab suggests the following:

375 g (13 oz) whole rolled oats
150 g (1 cup) sesame seeds
150 g (1 cup) sunflower seeds

75 g (½ cup) pumpkin seeds
250 g (1 cup) bee brood (*Apis mellifera*)
110 g (4 oz) honey
2 g (⅓ tsp) salt

Optional additions: birch sap, fennel seed, crushed juniper berry

Let bee brood thaw (if frozen). Blend in Thermomix with honey and salt. Stir the larvae-honey mixture into the seeds and grains and mix thoroughly. If desired, toss with some birch sap for added sweetness and clump ability. Then spread the mixture in a thin layer onto a tray and bake in a preheated oven at 160°C for 15–20 minutes.

Stir at minutes 5, 10, 13, 16 or as needed for even cooking.

For extra bee effect, mix in some dehydrated whole bee larvae for texture after granola is cooked and cooled.

Crunchy Silkworm Pupae (*Beondegi*)

From Kristofer Prepelica, 500 Tasty Sandwiches,
https://500sandwiches.com, used with permission

My friends who have tried silkworm pupae in Korea tell me they are tasty, but the canned pupae we find in the United States are practically inedible. The authors of the website 500 Tasty Sandwiches blame the taste on the canning process itself. They suggest that the off flavour can be eliminated by draining and soaking the canned pupae before using them.

1 × 4½ oz (130 g) can of silkworm pupae (*Bombyx mori*)
1 tbsp soy sauce
1 tbsp hot sauce
1 tsp sesame oil
2 garlic cloves, finely minced

Drain canned silkworm pupae and soak in cold water for one hour and repeat with fresh water twice more. After the last time, drain pupae and dry on a paper towel. Next, mix marinade.

Marinate pupae in sauce for 30 minutes. Line a baking sheet with parchment paper and preheat the oven to 400°F/205°C.

Drain the beondegi of excess marinade and evenly spread pupae on the baking sheet. Place in the oven and roast 45–60 minutes or until light and crisp. Give the baking sheet a shake every 10 minutes or so to ensure even roasting. When done, sprinkle salt to taste.

Thai Giant Water Bug Soup

This soup-for-two recipe comes from the Japanese author and ento-food enthusiast Mushimoiselle Giriko. The recipe was originally published in Giriko's book *Mushikui Noto* (Insect-tasting Notebook) and reprinted in the *Japan Times* on 14 December 2013; used with permission.

1 pickled water bug
4 okra
¼ onion
6 straw mushrooms
1 tsp chicken stock
2 cups (475 ml) water
½ lemon
pinch of Thai fish sauce and pepper
coriander (for serving)

Desalinate the water bug in water for about 1 hour, then make a cut on its abdomen. Cut okra into pieces, thinly slice onions and cut mushrooms in half. Boil water in pan. Add chicken stock and vegetables. Scrape out insides of the water bug into the pan when vegetables are cooked. Turn off heat, squeeze the lemon and add pepper and Thai fish sauce. Serve with coriander on top.

Insects *Tsukudani*

Tsukudani is a Japanese method of cooking and preserving small seafood, seaweed and meat, including insects that date from the Edo period. *Zazamushi*, or caddisfly larvae (see Chapter Four), and grasshoppers, or *inago*, are prepared *à la* tsukudani. This method could be used for a variety of insects. The result is a condiment used to accompany steamed rice.

To make *tsukudani* for about 150 g (1½ cups) of zazamushi (or mealworms), mix 3 tbsp sake, 3 tbsp dark soy sauce, 2 tbsp mirin and 2 tbsp of sugar. Soy sauce and sugar amounts can be adjusted to taste. Ginger, chillies or spices can be added for additional flavour.

First clean and dry insects. Stir-fry insects in a hot wok until cooked and dry.

In a heavy-bottomed pot, stir the sauce ingredients to combine, and add stir-fried insects. Bring to a low boil, and simmer until most of the liquid is absorbed and insects are candied. Store in the refrigerator.

Farofa de Iça (Ant Farofa)
Adapted from Ana Maria Brogui, www.anamariabrogui.com.br,
used with permission

The *iça* or *tanajura* ant, which includes various species of winged leafcutter ants (for example *Atta cephalotes*), are an age-old treat enjoyed by some rural populations in northeastern and southeastern Brazil. After a period of rains, the reproductive members of the nests swarm along the ground. People capture the winged adults – carefully, as the ants bite – and collect them in plastic bottles. The ants are prepared by removing the head, wings and legs. Only the large abdomens are used. A common way to eat them is to fry them together with toasted cassava meal and other ingredients to make a *farofa*, a popular countryside dish.

(amounts approximate)
150 g (1 cup) abdomens of winged adult leafcutter ants (for example *Atta cephalotes* or *A. sexdens*)

2 tbsp vegetable oil
1 small onion, chopped
300 g (2 cups) farinha (toasted cassava meal)
2 tbsp chopped fresh parsley
1 large tomato, chopped

Soak abdomens in warm salted water for 20 minutes. Remove the water. Fry in pan with oil for a few minutes to toast. Add onion and sauté.

Add toasted manioc farinha. Turn off heat and add tomatoes. Stir in parsley and serve.

The Missouri Entomophagist's Marinated June Bugs (or Japanese Beetle)
From Paul Landkamer, used with permission

Paul Landkamer is a Missouri master naturalist and editor of a Facebook group called Missouri Entomophagy. On request through the Missouri Entomophagy Facebook site, Mr Landkamer will share his text, *Dad's Cookbook: Being Some of the Recipes of Paul Landkamer, along with Other Stuff from My Culinary Experience* (2016 edition).

The following is based on Landkamer's basic recipe for marinated, dehydrated insects, which I have made with Japanese beetles (*Popillia japonica*) because they are so easy to collect.

Landkamer's Fish and Rice Sauce
Mix the following ingredients and let sit overnight

120 ml (½ cup) hot pepper sauce
60 ml (¼ cup) soy sauce
60 ml (¼ cup) water
150 g (¾ cup) sugar
4 tsp garlic powder
1 tsp ground ginger

1 tbsp cumin
1 tsp anise seed (optional)

Catch/acquire Japanese beetles in an area free of pesticides. (Adult beetles can infest new areas from several miles away but usually make only short flights as they move about to feed or lay eggs. Mine were harvested from a large, pesticide-free yard where they had heavily infested several rose bushes. Simply pick handfuls of beetles off the plants and throw into a bag.)

Freeze beetles to kill. Sort frozen insects to remove any leaves or debris, stray wings or parts. Boil insects for 5–10 minutes. Strain them from the water and fully submerge in marinade. Let them sit in marinade in the refrigerator overnight. Strain insects from the marinade and spread them in a single layer on dehydrator trays. Dry until crispy (about 6 hours for these).

References

Introduction

1 Arnold van Huis et al., *Edible Insects: Future Prospects for Food and Feed Security*, Food and Agriculture Organization of the United Nations, FAO Forestry Paper no. 171 (Rome, 2013).
2 United States Food and Drug Administration, *Food Defect Levels Handbook*, available online at www.fda.gov/food.
3 Van Huis et al., *Edible Insects*, p. 131.

1 Insects as Human Food

1 Peter Menzel and Faith D'Aluisio, *Man Eating Bugs: The Art and Science of Eating Insects* (Berkeley, CA, 1998), p. 174.
2 'Insect', Online Etymology Dictionary, www.etymonline. com, accessed 29 December 2019.
3 American Society of Mammalogists, Mammal Diversity Database, https://mammaldiversity.org, accessed 29 December 2018.
4 Eraldo M. Costa-Neto and Florence Dunkel, 'Insects as Food: History, Culture and Modern Use around the World', in *Insects as Sustainable Food Ingredients: Production, Processing and Food Applications*, ed. Aaron T. Dossey, Juan

A. Morales-Ramos and M. Guadalupe Rojas (London, 2016), p. 31.

5 Yde Jongema, 'List of Edible Insects of the World (1 April 2017)'. Online at www.wur.nl/en, accessed 29 December 2017.

6 Eraldo M. Costa-Neto and Julieta Ramos-Elorduy, 'Los insectos comestibles de Brasil. Etnicida, diversidad e importancia en la alimentacion', *Boletín Sociedad Entomológica Aragonesa*, No. 38 (2006), pp. 423–42.

7 Costa-Neto and Dunkel, 'Insects as Food', p. 29.

8 Lucinda R. Backwell and Francesco d'Errico, 'Evidence of Termite Foraging by Swartkrans Early Hominids', *Proceedings of the National Academy of Sciences of the United States of America*, XCVIII/4 (February 2001), pp. 1358–63.

9 William C. McGrew, 'The Other Faunivory: Primate Insectivory and Early Human Diet', in *Meat Eating and Human Evolution*, ed. Craig B. Stanford and Henry T. Bunn (Oxford, 2001), pp. 4–11.

10 Julie J. Lesnik, *Edible Insects and Human Evolution* (Gainesville, FL, 2018).

11 See, for example, Mark Q. Sutton, 'Insect Resources and Plio-Pleistocene Hominid Evolution', *Ethnobiology: Implication and Applications: Proceedings from the First International Conference of Ethnobiology, 1988*, 1 (Belém, 1990).

12 Lesnik, *Edible Insects*, p. 48.

13 Charlotte L. R. Payne et al., 'Are Edible Insects More or Less "Healthy" Than Commonly Consumed Meats? A Comparison Using Two Nutrient Profiling Models Developed to Combat Over- and Undernutrition', *European Journal of Clinical Nutrition*, LXX/3 (2015), pp. 285–91.

14 Charlotte L. R. Payne et al., 'A Systematic Review of Nutrient Composition Data Available for Twelve Commercially Available Edible Insects, and Comparison with Reference Values', *Trends in Food Science and Technology*, XLVII (2015), pp. 69–77.

15 Valerie J. Stull et al., 'Impact of Edible Cricket Consumption on Gut Microbiota in Healthy Adults: A Double-blind, Randomized Crossover Trial', *Scientific Reports*, XIII/10762 (2018), pp. 1–13.

16 David B. Madsen and James E. Kirkman, 'Hunting Hoppers', *American Antiquity*, LIII/3 (1988), pp. 593–604.

17 Frederick Simon Bodenheimer, *Insects as Human Food: A Chapter of the Ecology of Man* (The Hague, 1951).

18 Forkwas T. Fombong and John N. Kinyuru, 'Termites as Food in Africa', in *Termites and Sustainable Management*, Sustainability in Plant and Crop Protection series, vol. I, ed. M. A. Khan and W. Ahmad (New York, 2018), pp. 218–40.

19 Sandra G. F. Bukkens, 'The Nutritional Value of Edible Insects', *Ecology of Food and Nutrition*, XXXVI/2–4 (1997), pp. 287–320.

20 Arnold van Huis, 'Insects as Food in Sub-Saharan Africa', *Insect Science Application*, XXIII/3 (2003), pp. 163–85.

21 Fombong and Kinyuru, 'Termites', p. 234.

22 Ibid.

23 Rozzanna Esther Cavalcanti Reis de Figueirêdo et al., 'Edible and Medicinal Termites: A Global Overview', *Journal of Ethnobiology and Ethnomedicine*, XXXIIII/11 (2015), https://doi.org/10.1186/s13002-015-0016-4.

24 Pliny the Elder, *Natural History*, Book XXI, Chapter Four (London, 1855).

25 Eva Crane, *The Archaeology of Beekeeping* (Ithaca, NY, 1983).

26 Collin Turnbull, *The Forest People* (London, 1963).

27 'Vedda' is an antiquated term used to refer to the hunting and gathering peoples of Sri Lanka.

28 Bodenheimer, *Insects*, p. 249.

29 Ibid., p. 329.

30 Keith Allsop and J. Brand Miller, 'Honey Revisited: A Reappraisal of Honey in Pre-industrial Diets', *British Journal of Nutrition*, LXXV (1996), pp. 513–20.

31 Michael Cook and Susan Mineka, 'Selective Associations in the Observational Conditioning of Fear in Rhesus Monkeys', *Journal of Experimental Psychology: Animal Behavior Processes*, XVI/4 (1990), pp. 372–89.

32 Lesnik, *Edible Insects*, p. 20.

33 Jonathan Haidt et al., 'Body, Psyche, and Culture: The Relationship between Disgust and Morality', *Psychology and Developing Societies*, IX/1 (1997).

34 Gene R. Defoliart, 'Insects as Food: Why the Western Attitude Is Important', *Annual Review of Entomology*, XLIV (1999), p. 43.

35 Julie Lesnik, 'The Colonial/Imperial History of Insect Food Avoidance in the United States', *Annals of the Entomological Society of America*, CXII/6 (2019) pp. 560–65.

36 Marvin Harris, *Good to Eat* (Long Grove, IL, 1998 [1985]), p. 157.

2 A History of Insect Eating

1 Frederick Simon Bodenheimer, *Insects as Human Food: A Chapter of the Ecology of Man* (The Hague, 1951), pp. 15–6.

2 Jun Mitsuhashi, 'Entomophagy: Human Consumption of Insects', in *Encyclopedia of Entomology*, ed. John Capinera (Dordrecht, 2008).

3 Mark Q. Sutton, *Insects as Food: Aboriginal Entomophagy in the Great Basin* (Menlo Park, CA, 1988).

4 Matthew C, 'On the Significance of Insect Remains and Traces in Archaeological Interpretation', *Global Journal of Archaeology and Anthropology*, II/4 (January 2018), pp. 90–97.

5 Eraldo M. Costa-Neto and Florence Dunkel, 'Insects as Food: History, Culture and Modern Use around the World', in *Insects as Sustainable Food Ingredients: Production, Processing and Food Applications*, ed. Aaron T. Dossey, Juan A. Morales-Ramos and M. Guadalupe Rojas (London, 2016), p. 34.

6 May R. Berenbaum, *Bugs in the System: Insects and Their Impact on Human Affairs* (Reading, MA, 1995), p. 180.

7 Diodorus Siculus, *Library of History*, Loeb Classical Library edition, vol. II, Book III, Chapter 29 (Cambridge, MA, 1935), p. 163.

8 Joseph Bequaert, 'Insects as Food: How They Have Augmented the Food Supply of Mankind in Early and Recent Times', *Journal of the American Museum of Natural History* (March–April 1921), pp. 191–200, available at www.naturalhistorymag.com.

9 James Legge, *Sacred Books of the East*, XXVIII/Part 4: The Li Ki (1885), available at the Chinese Text Project, ctext.org/liji.

10 Lionel Wafer, *A New Voyage and Description of the Isthmus of America* (London, 1699), p. 67.

11 William Kirby and William Spence, *An Introduction to Entomology*, IV (1826), p. 300.

12 Vincent Holt, *Why Not Eat Insects?* (London, 1967 [1885]), p. 5.

13 Ronald Taylor, *Butterflies in My Stomach; or, Insects in Human Nutrition* (Santa Barbara, CA, 1971), p. 9.

14 Ibid., pp. 37–51.

15 V. B. Meyer-Rochow, 'Can Insects Help to Ease the Problem of World Food Shortage?', *Search*, VI/7 (1975), pp. 261–2.

16 Joshua Evans et al., '"Entomophagy": An Evolving Terminology in Need of Review', *Journal of Insects as Food and Feed*, 1/4 (2015), p. 295.

17 Ibid., pp. 296–300.

18 Peter Menzel and Faith D'Aluisio, *Man Eating Bugs: The Art and Science of Eating Insects* (Berkeley, CA, 1998), p. 144.

3 Feast or Famine

1 Based on news reports from Missouri, Kansas and Arkansas in 1875.

2 Chinua Achebe, *Things Fall Apart* (London, 1958).

3 Ibid., p 56.

4 Charles Valentine Riley, *The Locust Plague in the United States, Being More Particularly a Treatise on the Rocky Mountain Locust or So-Called Grasshopper, as It Occurs East of the Rocky Mountains, with Practical Recommendations for Its Destruction* (Chicago, IL, 1877), p. 39.

5 Charles Valentine Riley, *Report of the Commissioner of Agriculture for the Year 1877* (Washington, DC, 1878), p. 266.

6 Riley, *Locust*, p. 223.

7 Ibid., p. 224.

8 Other species, however, continue to have outbreaks that can cause severe agricultural damage. A devastating outbreak of the high plains grasshopper (*Dissosteira longipennis*), a borderline species, occurred in the 1930s, but has not occurred since because their population numbers are so low.

9 Jeffery A. Lockwood, *Locust: The Devastating Rise and Mysterious Disappearance of the Insect That Shaped the American Frontier* (New York, 2005).

10 Riley, *Locust*, p. 226.

11 Frederick Simon Bodenheimer, *Insects as Human Food: A Chapter of the Ecology of Man* (The Hague, 1951), p. 48.

12 Yupa Hamboonsong, 'Edible Insects and Associated Food Habits in Thailand', in *Edible Forest Insects* [Also *Forest Insects as Food*]: *Humans Bite Back!!*, ed. Patrick B. Durst et al. (Bangkok, 2010), pp. 173–4.

13 Jeffery H. Cohen, Nydia Delhi Mata Sánchez and Francisco Montiel-Ishino, 'Chapulines and Food Choices in Rural Oaxaca', *Gastronomica*, IX/1 (2009).

14 René Cerritos and Zenón Cano-Santana, 'Harvesting Grasshoppers *Sphenarium purpurascens* in Mexico for Human Consumption: A Comparison with Insecticidal

Control for Managing Pest Outbreaks, *Crop Protection*,
xxvii/3–5 (2008), pp. 473–80.

15 Hugh Raffles, *Insectopedia* (New York, 2010), p. 14.

16 Ibid., p. 227.

4 Rustling Up Some Grub(s) around the World

1 Quoted in Frederick Simon Bodenheimer, *Insects as Human
Food: A Chapter of the Ecology of Man* (The Hague, 1951),
p. 72.

2 Alan Louey Yen, 'Edible Insects and Other Invertebrates
in Australia: Future Prospects', in *Edible Forest Insects*
[also *Forest Insects as Food*]: *Humans Bite Back!!*, ed. Patrick
B. Durst et al. (Bangkok, 2010), p. 67.

3 Peter Menzel and Faith D'Aluisio, *Man Eating Bugs:
The Art and Science of Eating Insects* (New York, 1998), p. 18.

4 Aung Si and Myfany Turpin, 'The Importance of Insects
in Australian Aboriginal Society: A Dictionary Survey',
Ethnobiology Letters, vi/1 (2015), pp. 175–82.

5 For more information see www.cultureandrecreation.gov.au.

6 Luo Zhi-Yi, 'Insects as Traditional Food in China', in
Ecological Implications of Minilivestock, ed. Maurizio Paoletti
(Enfield, nh, 2005), pp. 475–80.

7 Andy Deemer, 'Why Do Chinese People Eat Snakes, Ants,
and Worms for Medicine?', *The World of Chinese* (2010),
online at www.theworldofchinese.com, accessed 26
October 2020.

8 Luo Zhi-Yi, 'Insects as Traditional Food in China', p. 478.

9 V. B. Meyer-Rochow, 'Traditional Food Insects and Spiders
in Several Ethnic Groups of Northeast India, Papua and
New Guinea, Australia, and New Zealand', in *Ecological
Implications of Mini Livestock – Potential of Insects, Rodents,
Frogs and Snails*, ed. M. G. Paoletti (Enfield, ct, 2005),
pp 385–409.

10 Lobeno Mozhui, L. N. Kakati, Patricia Kiewhuo and Sapu
Changkija, 'Traditional Knowledge of the Utilization of

Edible Insects in Nagaland, North-east India', *Foods*, ix/7 (2020), article number 852.

11 Kenichi Nonaka, 'Cultural and Commercial Roles of Edible Wasps in Japan', in *Edible Forest Insects*, pp. 123–30.

12 Julieta Ramos-Elorduy, 'The Importance of Edible Insects in the Nutrition and Economy of People in Rural Areas of Mexico', *Ecology of Food and Nutrition*, xxxvi/5 (1997), pp. 336–47.

13 Ibid., p. 47.

14 Mark Q. Sutton, *Insects as Food: Aboriginal Entomophagy in the Great Basin* (Menlo Park, ca, 1988).

15 Rudzani Makhado et al., 'A Review of the Significance of Mopane Products to Rural People's Livelihoods in Southern Africa', *Transactions of the Royal Society of South Africa*, lxix/2 (2014), pp. 117–22; usaid, 'Mopane Worm for Improved Income Generation (mw4iig) Innovation', online at www.ranlab.org, accessed 6 January 2018.

16 William S. Bristowe, 'Insects and Other Invertebrates for Human Consumption in Siam', *Transactions of the Entomological Society of London*, lxxx/2 (1932), p. 394.

17 Andrew Müller, 'Insects as Food in Laos and Thailand: A Case of "Westernisation"?', *Asian Journal of Social Science*, xlvii (2019), pp. 204–23.

5 Rearing Mini-livestock

1 Gene DeFoliart, 'Edible Insects as Minilivestock', *Biodiversity and Conservation*, ix (1995), p. 306.

2 Ibid.

3 Yuxuan Gong et al., 'Biomolecular Evidence of Silk from 8,500 Years Ago', *PLoS ONE*, xi/12 (2016).

4 Frederick Simon Bodenheimer, *Insects as Human Food: A Chapter of the Ecology of Man* (The Hague, 1951), p. 271.

5 Ibid., p. 275.

6 Thomas Lecocq, 'Insects: The Disregarded Domestication Histories', in *Animal Domestication*, ed. Fabrice Telechea

(2019), pp. 35–68, available at www.intechopen.com, accessed 2 November 2020.

7   Annette Bruun Jensen et al., 'Standard Methods for *Apis mellifera* Brood as Human Food', *Journal of Apicultural Research*, LVIII/2 (2019), pp. 1–28.

8   Sarah Kobylewski and Michael F. Jacobson, 'Toxicology of Food Dyes', *International Journal of Occupational and Environmental Health*, XVIII/3 (July–September, 2012), pp. 220–46.

9   Nancy Shute, 'Is That a Crushed Bug in Your Frothy Starbucks Drink?', *The Salt* blog, NPR [National Public Radio] (30 March 2012).

10 S. Kelemu et al., 'African Edible Insects for Food and Feed: Inventory, Diversity, Commonalities and Contribution to Food Security', *Journal of Insects as Food and Feed*, 1/2 (2015), p. 110.

11 Darna L. Dufour and Joy B. Sander, 'II.G.15/Insects', in *The Cambridge World History of Food*, ed. Kenneth F. Kiple and Kriemhild Coneé Ornelas, vol. 1 (Cambridge, 2000), p. 549.

12 Francisco Hernández, 1959 [1576], *História natural de Nueva España*, cited in Jeffrey R. Parsons, 'The Aquatic Component of Aztec Subsistence: Hunters, Fishers, and Collectors in an Urbanized Society', *Michigan Discussions in Anthropology* (issue title: *Subsistence and Sustenance*), XV/1 (2005), pp. 61–2.

13 Joost van Itterbeeck and Arnold van Huis, 'Environmental Manipulation for Edible Insect Procurement: A Historical Perspective', *Journal of Ethnobiology and Ethnomedicine*, XVIII/3 (2010), p. 3.

14 Jeffrey R. Parsons, 'The Aquatic Component of Aztec Subsistence: Hunters, Fishers, and Collectors in an Urbanized Society', *Michigan Discussions in Anthropology* (issue title: *Subsistence and Sustenance*), XV/1 (2005), p. 64.

15 Van Itterbeeck and Van Huis, 'Environmental Manipulation', pp. 3–4.

16 Mark S. Hoddle, 'Entomophagy: Farming Palm Weevils for Food', Center for Invasive Species Research (CISR) blog (30 September 2013).

17 Van Itterbeeck and van Huis, 'Environmental Manipulation', p. 4.

18 Charlotte L. R. Payne et al., 'The Contribution of "Chitoumou", the Edible Caterpillar *Cirina butyrospermi*, to the Food Security of Smallholder Farmers in Southwestern Burkina Faso', *Food Security*, XII/1 (2020), pp. 221–34.

19 Patrick Durst and Kenichi Shono, 'Edible Forest Insects: Exploring New Horizons and Traditional Practices', in *Edible Forest Insects* [also *Forest Insects as Food*]: *Humans Bite Back!!*, ed. Patrick B. Durst et al. (Bangkok, 2010), p. 1.

20 Katherine Harmon, 'Mealworms: The Other-other-other White Meat', *Scientific American* (19 December 2012).

21 See Arnold van Huis, Henk van Gurp and Marcel Dicke, *The Insect Cookbook: Food for a Sustainable Planet* (New York, 2014).

22 Afton Halloran et al., 'The Development of the Edible Cricket Industry in Thailand', *Journal of Insects as Food and Feed*, II/2 (2016), pp. 91–100.

23 Talal Husseini, 'Thailand Published Cricket Farming Good Agricultural Practice Rules', *Food Processing Technology* (19 March 2019).

24 'Glimpse inside the Largest Human Grade Cricket Farm in the World', https://entonation.com (28 January 2018).

25 As of January 2018, as stated on https://entomofarms.com.

26 Elaine Watson, 'Aspire Food Group Unveils World's First Automated Cricket Farm', *FoodNavigator-USA* (4 August 2017).

27 Mark E. Lundy and Michael P. Parella, 'Crickets Are Not a Free Lunch: Protein Capture from Scalable Organic Side-streams via High-density Populations of *Acheta domesticus*', *PLoS ONE*, X/4 (2015).

28 Stephen Chen, 'A Giant Indoor Farm in China Is Breeding 6 Billion Cockroaches a Year. Here's Why', *South China Morning Post* (19 April 2018).

29 Christopher Ingraham, 'Maggots: A Taste of Food's Future', *Washington Post* (3 July 2019).

6 The Insectivore's Dilemma

1 See Kate Andrews, 'Farm 432: Insect Breeding by Katharina Unger', www.dezeen.com (25 July 2013).

2 Ophelia Deroy, Ben Reade and Charles Spence, 'The Insectivore's Dilemma, and How to Take the West out of it', *Food Quality and Preference*, XLIV (2015), pp. 44–55.

3 Ibid.

4 Ibid., p. 135.

5 Taken from Alex Atala, *D.O.M.: Rediscovering Brazilian Ingredients* (London, 2013), p. 38.

6 Nordic Food Lab, Joshua Evans, Roberto Flore and Michael Bom Frøst, *On Eating Insects: Essays, Stories and Recipes* (London, 2017), pp. 314–15.

7 Daniella Martin, *Edible: An Adventure into the World of Eating Insects and the Last Great Hope to Save the Planet* (Boston, MA, 2014).

8 See Andrew Müller's blog, at http://contemporaryfoodlab.com.

9 A. Müller et al., 'Entomophagy and Power', *Journal of Insects as Food and Feed*, II/2 (2016).

10 See Alex Atala's ATA Institute website, at www.institutoata.org.br, my translation.

11 Ibid., my translation.

12 Francisco Sánchez-Bayo and Kris A. G. Wyckhuys, 'Worldwide Decline of the Entomofauna: A Review of Its Drivers', *Biological Conservation*, CCXXXII (2019), pp. 8–27.

Select Bibliography

Bodenheimer, Frederick Simon, *Insects as Human Food: A Chapter of the Ecology of Man* (The Hague, 1951)

Dossey, Aaron T., Juan A. Morales-Ramos and M. Guadalupe Rojas, eds, *Insects as Sustainable Food Ingredients: Production, Processing and Food Applications* (London, 2016)

Durst, Patrick B., et al., eds, *Edible Forest Insects* [also *Forest Insects as Food*]: *Humans Bite Back!!* (Bangkok, 2010)

Nordic Food Lab, Joshua Evans, Roberto Flore and Michael Bom Frøst, *On Eating Insects: Essays, Stories and Recipes* (London, 2017)

Lesnik, Julie J., *Edible Insects and Human Evolution* (Gainesville, FL, 2018)

Menzel, Peter, and Faith D'Aluisio, *Man Eating Bugs: The Art and Science of Eating Insects* (Berkeley, CA, 1998)

Van Huis, Arnold, Henk van Gurp and Marcel Dicke, *The Insect Cookbook: Food for a Sustainable Planet* (New York, 2014)

—, et al., *Edible Insects: Future Prospects for Food and Feed Security*, Food and Agriculture Organization of the United Nations, FAO Forestry Paper no. 171 (Rome, 2013)

Walter-Toews, David, *Eat the Beetles: An Exploration into Our Conflicted Relationship with Insects* (Toronto, 2017)

Websites and Associations

BugsFeed
www.bugsfeed.com

Eat Grub
www.eatgrub.co.uk

EntoMarket
www.edibleinsects.com

Food and Agriculture Organization of the United Nations
www.fao.org

Little Herds
www.littleherds.org

North American Coalition for Insect Agriculture
https://nacia.org

Thailand Unique
www.thailandunique.com

Acknowledgements

It took me a long time to write this short book. I wrote it in fits and starts as I took up different aspects of the long and multifaceted history of edible insects. To paraphrase Henry David Thoreau, it is not that the story needed to be long, but it took a while to make it short. I have barely scratched the surface of the topic here; the sheer diversity of insects and insect foods continues to amaze me. I hope the scholars of the field will forgive the inevitable omissions and any entomological errors that I have made.

Thanks to Andrew F. Smith, series editor; Michael R. Leaman, publisher; editor Amy Salter; and all the staff at Reaktion Books for making this book possible. Thanks to all the researchers and writers, too numerable to mention here but many cited in the text, who responded to my random requests for information, recipes, photos and resources.

I thank my dear friend and colleague James Skibo, who first encouraged me to write the book; and the Department of Sociology and Anthropology at Illinois State University for the supportive, collegial environment they have provided over the years. Thanks to Amber Bostwick, also at Illinois State, for her helpful editorial work on early drafts of some chapters; and to Sarah Dick at Milner Library for her incredibly helpful copyright assistance.

I owe huge thanks to the many people who bring me joy. To my crew, who warm my heart with their care and my belly with their cooking: Chris Koos, Lucille Eckrich and especially Lulu

(Maria Luisa) Zamudio, my bug-eating, travelling compañera. To mom and dad (Jim and Linda Hunter) and my sisters (Joy Merino, Eva Hunter, Cassandra Porter) for their unwavering support and for not asking too often if the book was done yet. To Filipe, Natalie and Lua Bessa (and the one on the way) for being my family; and to my Love, Douglas Biever, for being my ally, abettor and favourite distraction.

This book is dedicated to the indigenous people of the world, from whom there is so much to learn.

Photo Acknowledgements

The author and publishers wish to express their thanks to the below sources of illustrative material and/or permission to reproduce it.

Alamy: pp. 10 (World History Archive), 70 (Penny Tweedie), 77 (Terry Allen), 92 (Jatuphot Phuatawee), 101 (agefotostock), 103 (Andy Harmer); Centre of Geo Information by Ron van Lammeren, Wageningen University, The Netherlands, based on data compiled by Yde Jongema, 2017: p. 18 top (www.wur.nl/en/Research-Results/Chair-groups/Plant-Sciences/Laboratory-of-Entomology/Edible-insects/Worldwide-species-list.htm); Cooper Hewitt, Smithsonian Design Museum, New York: p. 8; Gina Hunter: pp. 11, 66, 83, 97, 108, 112, 124, 127, 128, 129, 130; Yde Jongema, 2017, Department of Entomology of Wageningen University & Research, The Netherlands: p. 18 centre (www.wur.nl); Kansas Historical Society, Topeka p. 52; Rubens Kato (used with permission): p. 122; Ryo Koine (used with permission): p. 80; Little Herds (www.littleherds.org): p. 109; Minneapolis Museum of Art: p. 9; Musée de la Chartreuse de *Douai*: p. 40; Kenichi Nonaka (used with permission): p. 81 top; Nutrition table: p. 25. Data adapted from Charlotte L. R. Payne, Pete Scarborough, M. Rayner, and K. Nonaka 'Are edible insects more or less "healthy" than commonly consumed meats? A comparison using two nutrient profiling models developed to combat over- and undernutrition.' *European Journal of Clinical Nutrition*, XVII/3, pp. 285–91; V. B. Meyer-Rochow (used

them online under conditions imposed by a Creative Commons Attribution-Share Alike 3.0 Unported License. Achillea: p. 38. Drawing of a painting from the caves of Cueva de la Araña by fr:Utilisateur:Achillea converted to svg by User:Amada44. This work is free software; you can redistribute it and/or modify it under the terms of the GNU General Public License as published by the Free Software Foundation; either version 2 of the License, or any later version. This work is distributed in the hope that it will be useful, but without any warranty; without even the implied warranty of merchantability or fitness for a particular purpose. HTO, the copyright holder of the image on p. 39, has released this work into the public domain. This applies worldwide. Picture taken by en:User:Diomidis Spinellis on mountain in Ymittos, Greece: p. 41. Transferred from en.wikipedia to Commons. The original uploader was Diomidis Spinellis at English Wikipedia. This file is licensed under the Creative Commons Attribution-Share Alike 3.0 Unported License. starwarzallegro: p. 46. This file is from Pixabay, where the creator has released it explicitly under the license Creative Commons Zero. This file, which was originally posted to Pixabay, was reviewed on 17 July 2017 by reviewer Speravir, who confirmed that it was available on Pixabay on that date. This file is made available under the Creative Commons CC0 1.0 Universal Public Domain Dedication. Shardan, the copyright holder of the image on p. 48, has published it online under conditions imposed by a Creative Commons Attribution-Share Alike 2.5 Generic License. Modified from Burrows, Rogers, Ott; DOI: 10.1186/2042-1001-1-11 (desert locust image): p. 54. The image was first formally published as part of a figure (Fig. 1A) in a review article of Burrows, M., Rogers, S. M. and Ott, S.R. 'Epigenetic remodelling of brain, body and behaviour during phase change in locusts', *Neural Syst Circ*, 1/11 (2011), https://dx.doi.org/10.1186/2042-1001-1-11. This is an Open Access article distributed under the terms of the Creative Commons Attribution License, which permits unrestricted use, distribution, and reproduction in any medium, provided the original work is properly cited. User:Sputnikcccp: p. 72 (Permission: GFDL.) Permission is granted to copy, distribute and/or modify this document under the terms of the GNU Free Documentation

Index

italic numbers refer to illustrations; **bold** to recipes